The
EASY GARDEN

Month-by-Month

The
EASY GARDEN

Month-by-Month

MICHAEL JEFFERSON-BROWN

David & Charles

A DAVID & CHARLES BOOK

Copyright © Michael Jefferson-Brown 1995
First published 1995
Reprinted 1995
Reprinted 1996 (twice)
Paperback edition 1998

A catalogue record for this book is available from the British
Library.

ISBN 0 7153 0228 0 (hardback)
ISBN 0 7153 0710 X (paperback)

Illustrations by Avis Murray
Book design by Diana Knapp

Typeset by ABM Typographics Ltd, Hull
and printed in Italy
by New Interlitho Italia
for David & Charles
Brunel House   Newton Abbot   Devon

CONTENTS

INTRODUCTION

The vicar leaning over the gate: 'Hello George, you and the Almighty have made a wonderful job tending the garden.' The reply: 'Thank 'ee vicar, but you should have see'd it when He was doing it Hisself.'

It is an old story but there is a grain of truth lurking there. No garden manages itself without some effort – even if you get a ready-mix concrete lorry to drop a load and cover all, it is going to need sweeping periodically. But, and this is a heavyweight 'but', some fine gardens can be made and kept in attractive shape with a lot less effort than others. There are things that can be done to avoid continual labour, there are ideas to be adopted and others to be shunned, and there are design possibilities that delight without needing much maintenance.

HOW EASY IS EASY?

'Easy' is, of course, a relative term. Here we have adopted it on behalf of all those gardeners who have no ambitions to turn their plot into a green-style torture chamber. Instead, we picture our ideal garden more as a haven of peace and quiet where we can refresh ourselves amongst a riot of beauty, enjoying the colours and scents of the flowers, the glorious foliage and the architectural lines of the contrasting plants, almost deafened by the bird song and contemplating nature in perfect harmony.

Complete idleness could, perhaps, be the ideal of a few. For these the easy garden will be one where others do the work, and in this respect it is as well to bear in mind the dictum that you should never start on a garden that is bigger than your partner can manage!

SEASONS AND MONTHS

Under average conditions, the terms 'early', 'mid' and 'late' season as used throughout the book correspond to the following months:

WINTER
Early: December
Mid: January
Late: February

SPRING
Early: March
Mid: April
Late: May

SUMMER
Early: June
Mid: July
Late: August

AUTUMN
Early: September
Mid: October
Late: November

(opposite) *Foliage can be important at all times, but so can the inanimate. Boulders and pebbles can be a lively part of the landscape, especially if combined with water. Here is variegated grass with* Ligularia 'Rocket', *the variegated flag iris* (Iris pseudacoris variegata) *and hostas*

Late-spring paeony 'Bowl of Beauty' once planted will perform annually for the next fifty years with the very minimum of care

The introduction to each chapter deals with the character of a particular month and highlights some of the plants that can be expected to be at their best at that time. Tasks for the Month then covers jobs that will need attention, giving ideas and suggestions as to how they can best be completed.

Each month, plants are recommended that will more or less look after themselves. Some have been highlighted as Plants of the Month; these are usually supported by lists of excellent substitutes or companions. In many cases there are more details about these in the Appendices at the back of the book.

With such a wealth of plants now available to gardeners, the choice presented here is simply our selection. Most certainly you could create a wonderful garden with only some of these recommended kinds, while many hugely different gardens could be created using exactly the same choice – once again, it is one of the many joys of gardening that there are no exact rules, and that everyone can experiment in their own way. Perhaps we can be guided away from making obvious mistakes, but some of the happiest effects in our gardens may be almost accidental. The emphasis in our selection, though, is on shrubs, naturalising bulbs, ground cover and unfussy perennial plants, which will be the backbone and much of the flesh of the easy garden.

'EASY' PLANT TYPES

Evergreen trees and shrubs

Tidy deciduous trees such as decorative crab apples *(Malus)*, flowering cherries, rowans and whitebeams *(Sorbus)*, silver birches *(Betula)* and the stronger maples *(Acer)*

Most of the hardy deciduous shrubs

Bulbs that can be left 'naturalised' in the ground for years such as many daffodils, bluebells, martagon lilies, *Nerine bowdenii* and then the little ones – crocuses, chionodoxas, cyclamens, snowdrops, and winter aconites

Persistent perennials such as herbaceous paeonies, rudbeckias, doronicums, and shasta daisies, and foliage plants such as hostas and rodgersias

For those who would be real gardeners, though, this book aims to suggest some of the garden planning, making of garden features and plants that can be used to create a very satisfying garden that may be enjoyed for decades. It is not suggested that this will be achieved without effort, rather that the garden can provide a place of enjoyment and require just the amount of work that will be pleasurable without making its creator a slave to its demands.

PICK AND CHOOSE

In many spheres of endeavour the rules and regimes laid down by the 'experts' are, or can be treated as, merely suggestions or the prejudices of their proponents. It is certainly so in the garden, and we do not have to follow the 'rules'. Fashions change, whether in design or in the popularity of a particular type of plant, and as gardeners we can pick and choose; in this book you are *expected* to pick and choose.

Every garden will be an individual creation. If a hundred gardeners were given an identical set of plants and ready-made features, the results would be a hundred different gardens. Sites vary, household requirements differ and each person is going to aim at somewhat different results. This book is a mass of suggestions: the reader picks and mixes.

Each month includes one, and sometimes two, practical projects. We do not expect any one reader to follow through all the projects in sequence within the year – though perhaps we ought to consider a 'gardener of the year' award for anyone who does! Rather, the projects are detailed to show how certain attractive features might be introduced into the scheme of things, be constructed with the minimum of labour and expense, and then be kept in order without too much toil and trouble.

A garden is not static: it develops and changes over the years. As time goes by, and muscles become less forceful and energy less plentiful, it makes sense to plan a garden that, once established, will not require too much work. The double digging of a vegetable patch, for example, may be enjoyable for a number of years, but can then become drudgery and, finally, an impossible torture. The idea is to plan a garden where flower and fruit delight, and where plant life and designed structures provide peace and just enough gentle work as to be truly recreational. Most gardeners have neither the space or time for a vegetable garden. It is not easy gardening. The same applies to most fruits, though apples and pears can be very decorative in blossom and productive when established. Cherries are glorious in blossom; the birds get the fruit.

GARDEN ECOLOGY: GARDEN SENSE

Nowadays, the word ecology keeps popping up, and we are all concerned with our threatened environment – and indeed our threatened world. Our own garden is a tiny part of the jigsaw, and in it we are caring for and creating an environment. From a bare site, each plant or structure we introduce will slightly alter the balance. We are constantly creating and modifying microclimates, so that particular spots become either better or less happy homes for certain plants.

There are particular groups of plants that seem to look right together and grow in harmony, and these associations can help to formulate the changing character of the garden. As the year passes different groups of plants come into prominence, and our easy garden can capitalise on such happy groupings so that we find ourselves looking forward to repeat performances as the new year beckons. It is our plants we see first, but of course the birds and other wildlife can be very much encouraged to join us.

There are no laws that say you must garden. It is for enjoyment, and this book is offered in the hope that enjoyment may be made fuller and especially that it should extend throughout the year. A garden that ceases to be attractive after the first frosts of the autumn and is open for business again only when the daffodils bloom is, by this definition, not a true garden. This book looks at the easy garden month by month, focusing our attention so that, hopefully, we can make the most of our patch not only each month but day by day.

9

JANUARY

A look into the garden in the depths of winter reveals whether or not we have managed to create an all-year-round garden. The design is laid bare. We see the infrastructure, the walls, paths and buildings as well as the pergolas, screens and garden ornaments. Deciduous shrubs and trees are silhouettes, and afford a contrast to the evergreens that take on an even more important role in the overall plan.

Now more than ever we are able to appreciate the interplay of shapes: the lines of deciduous plants and of path and border edges against the masses of conifers – green and gold – and the comforting bulk of clipped hedges. Colour may be added by the rusted brown of beech.

The higher structures are more noticeable now than in the summer; then there is hectic activity close to the ground, herbaceous plants and shrubs extrovertly calling attention to themselves. Now we see trees reaching for the skies, spreading wide-armed above. The arched pergola suggests shelter, as well as making a determined effort to haul down some of the space above our heads into the garden design. Gravelled or grassed areas take on added importance, as do the heathers that may be in bloom for months. Colour and mass work together. Apart from conifers there are the other evergreens: the hollies, especially the variegated ones, the humble but worthy golden privet and the gleaming Elaeagnus pungens 'Maculata', with its wide, golden-painted variegation shining bright in winter sunshine. Dark evergreen masses may be highlighting the splendid blossom of yellow witch hazels, the Hamamelis. One winter-blooming bush is worth a forest of summer ones; it makes sense to make the most of our winter stars.

tasks
FOR THE
month

CHECKLIST ✓

- Carry out maintenance work on garden tools
- Order/purchase seeds
- Join societies
- Draw up plans for your garden

ESSENTIAL TOOLS

Spade }
Fork } **preferably stainless steel**

Rake, wide
Trowel
Secateurs
Sprayer
Watering can/hose

IN LARGER GARDENS
Wheelbarrow
Lawnmower

TOOL MAINTENANCE

Life is easier if tools are kept in good order and live in a designated place. A few really good, well-cared-for tools, stored sensibly, are far more useful than a haphazard collection including gadgets made for every possible specific task. Tools can become old friends and seem extensions of one's own body; you hardly notice their independent existence when working. Stainless steel trowels and spades can last decades, their initial high cost being repaid time after time in ease of use, ease of maintenance and pleasure in ownership.

After you have finished using your tools, clean off any soil and plant debris and store them in a shed or garage. Most can be hung on the wall out of the way. Ultra-tidy gardeners might like to paint the outlined shape of tools on the shed walls so that each has its own berth but a hook or nail is probably enough.

With the weather often preventing work in the garden, now is a sensible time to check all those tools with cutting edges and mechanical parts, so that reliable servicing can be completed well before they will be in use again. Grass cutters, secateurs and saws need inspecting and should be left lightly oiled after sharpening and cleaning. There are simple tools on sale at garden centres and elsewhere which can be used for efficient sharpening, although the cost of having the job done professionally is not usually exorbitant.

Abandon any tools that are hopelessly broken or unlikely to be used again, and dispose of those gadgets which were going to save so much time and effort but proved next to useless.

ORDERING/BUYING SEEDS

The emphasis in this book is not on raising huge numbers of bedding plants – that way lies work, not the easy garden. However, you may wish to try some new things each year and repeat successful ideas, perhaps a screen of sweet peas or some other annual feature.

It is often easier, and sometimes cheaper, to buy young seedlings in two or three months' time than to go to the trouble of raising your own (see p20 and 40). Some annuals are so easy that, after being introduced into the garden initially, they will reproduce themselves year by year; love-in-the-mist, for example, will be with you forever if allowed to seed (see p113).

Perennials of particular interest can be raised economically from seed. Specialist mail-order firms produce interesting seed catalogues, but most garden centres also provide a very extensive range.

JOINING SOCIETIES

Apart from the social benefits, there are other big advantages to society memberships. Subscriptions are usually very modest indeed; local clubs often have a monthly programme of meetings with specialist speakers and also arrange shows and competitions. They usually send in combined seed orders and offer considerable discounts for members. Join now. See Useful Addresses for other organisations.

GARDEN PLANNING

Designing for ease
Access to all parts of the garden is essential for the gardener and his tools: if there is grass to be mown, for example, there needs to be an easy run for the mower from the storage quarters to the grass.

A compost area should be out of sight, but easily approached with a barrow. A very modest garden may manage with a manufactured bin; larger gardens will require a space at least 2 x 1m (6 x 3ft) (see p28). Shredders used to reduce hedge clippings and other garden rubbish to a useful mulch or composting material are compact, but a working space of 2–3 sq m (2–3 sq yd) will be needed. These machines are becoming much more popular, but before you purchase one be sure that you have enough work to make it economical, and then make sure that you choose the most appropriate one – and one that is reliable and safe. Larger gardens may include areas for bonfires to deal with material that cannot be composted or easily carted to a tip.

Pathways should look pleasant and be strong enough not to be damaged by a loaded barrow. Whilst the paths have to look in sensible proportion to the garden size and design, a working path needs to be a minimum width of 75cm (30in) and will be safer at 1m (3ft). Pathways made of stone, brick, slabs, gravel or other materials, as opposed to grass, should require the minimum of maintenance. Initially, this will probably entail providing a good hardcore base, and later, making sure that they are kept free of weeds and surplus water at all times (see p44).

Lawns

The advantages and disadvantages of lawns are dealt with in this month's practical project. Lawn edges will need almost as much attention as the rest of the lawn, so it is sensible to make these easy to look after as well as attractive.

Garden centres sell lightweight metal edging, usually with a wavy outline to gain strength. Using this makes the lawn edges less vulnerable to being broken down and easier to keep neatly trimmed.

A stone or brick path between borders and lawn can look impressive, strengthening design lines and cutting out the need to look after lawn edges.

WARNING

■ *If metal lawn edging is used, it is essential that the upper surface is level and cannot be touched by grass cutters, otherwise dangerous jagged edges can be created that may cause serious injuries* ■

ENCOURAGING WILDLIFE

■ *Plant plenty of cover as trees and shrubs. Easy trees could include:*
Acer campestre, FIELD MAPLE
Betula pendula, SILVER BIRCH
Ilex aquifolium, HOLLY
Malus sylvestris, CRAB APPLE
Sorbus aria, WHITEBEAM
S. acuparia, ROWAN

■ *Put up nest boxes.*

■ *Provide winter bird-feeding tables.*

■ *Have water available in bird baths or an accessible pond.*

■ *Do not be too tidy in the borders: let some leaf and wood litter lie.*

■ *Allow seeding plants and ornamental grasses to remain and provide food sources.*

Designs and plans

Sketch the main areas of gravel, patio, paths, borders and beds, and then mark these out on the ground itself. This can be done easily using hosepipes, rope and string to delineate some of the features, while stones, wood and even cardboard can be used to give some feel of their real shape and size. In this way you will discover whether something that looks possible and right on paper is obviously wrong on the ground.

Plans are not works of art. Keep everything simple. Shapes should be as bold as possible, lacking fussiness. If edges are not straight, the curves need to be obvious but generous, so that the eye is led gently and the mowing machine can follow easily. Give the main features such as pergolas, screens and trees their places early, even if they are not built or planted in the garden for months or years. It is a very good idea to live with the main lines of the design for a while before committing yourself to physical work – modifications will suggest themselves,

some purely aesthetic, others practical.

The obvious things can get overlooked. The garden is going to be viewed mostly from the house, probably from the main living room and kitchen, and it should look as good as possible from these viewpoints. Most gardens are used partly as an extension of the house, perhaps as an 'outdoor room'. A patio area adjoining or close to the house may serve this purpose well, so that you can move outside on to hardstanding and find a place to sit at ease. It needs to be sheltered and to enjoy at least some periods of sunshine.

From the house the eye will be drawn to various features, and it is pleasant to be intrigued visually by suggestions of vistas beyond. Certainly a feeling of space needs to be created and eyesores hidden as far as possible. False perspectives can be used to enhance a feeling of length, rectangular lawns or gravelled ways becoming narrower in the distance, and the same ploy can be used with paths and pergolas.

OTHER JOBS

Choose a frost-free day to spray top fruit (apples, pears, etc), using tar-oil wash to kill insect pests, their eggs and green lichen – after pruning away dead, diseased and weak wood.

Knock heavy piles of snow from evergreen shrubs and trees.

Keep houseplants in light, cool places and water only when the soil is nearly dry.

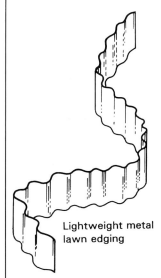

Lightweight metal lawn edging

plants
OF THE
month

WITCH HAZEL
(Hamamelis mollis)

Witch hazels are very exciting, true winter-blooming shrubs, gaining in impact as they grow year by year and needing no special attention. They are very hardy, originating in China and North America. The leading species is the Chinese *Hamamelis mollis*, but there is now a wide range of winter-flowering hybrids varying in flower colour from lemon and gold to tawny, orange, mahogany and dark red. All are excellent, but the yellows show up more brightly from a distance. Flowers are arranged on bare twigs, the petals like mini-ribboning. The blossom is very cold resistant and lasts for many weeks.

type	Hardy, open, spreading shrub
size	Height and spread 3.5m (12ft)
foliage	Deciduous, large hazel-like leaves 10–15cm (4–6in) long, mid-green turning golden in autumn
flowers	Fragrant, rich yellow blossom clasped on twigs of the current year's growth in early to mid winter. Petals are narrow strips 2cm (¾in) long

HAMAMELIS MOLLIS

site	The showy winter flower colour is seen best against a dark background such as holly or conifers
soil	Grows in a wide variety of soils, but best in a well-drained, good loam and benefits from humus when newly planted
care	Avoid deep cultivation once established. Leaf mulches are appreciated
propagation	Commercially, witch hazels are usually propagated by grafting pieces on seedlings of *Hamamelis virginiana*. In the garden, air layering is slowish but sure. Some seasons the shrubs produce crops of 'nuts', each usually containing four seeds. If these are sown in pots they can be left outside to be frosted and will germinate in spring. Seedlings of hybrids will not come true to their parent but will be worth having, although it will take perhaps 4–5 years before the first blooms appear
varieties	See margin

COTONEASTER
(Cotoneaster × watereri)

A series of fine fruiting, evergreen bushes have been derived from *Cotoneaster frigida* and *C. henryana*. All are characterised by the heavy crops of rich red, bunched fruits that they hang out very decoratively from autumn through the winter. These seem to hold minimal interest for birds that will strip bare hollies and other cotoneasters in no time.

type	Wide-spreading and arching shrub or small tree
size	Height 3-4.5m (10-15ft), spread 4.5m (15ft)
foliage	Evergreen, spear-shaped leaves 4-8cm (1½-3in) long, dark green
flowers and fruit	Wide heads of small white flowers in early summer. Conspicuous large bunches of round, deep red, persistent fruits are very freely produced
site	Can be grown wherever its evergreen status and long-lasting fruit is best appreciated, perhaps in places where the fruits can be seen against the sky. Grows strongly so give ample space
care	Extremely hardy and vigorous, the removal of lower branches and a little support for a leading growth

can start the conversion of a bush into a small tree

propagation By cuttings in late summer or layers in autumn. Seed germinates freely and the seedlings grow exceedingly quickly into substantial plants. These can be raised by simply covering a few berries in the open ground. The resulting plants will vary, but within very restricted limits

cultivars 'Avonbank', 'Cornubia', 'Goscote' and 'John Waterer' are similar. 'Pendulus' is as free fruiting but is markedly weeping

GARRYA
(Garrya elliptica)

A dark, evergreen shrub grown for its freely borne, long catkins of silver-grey carried as festooned decoration throughout the winter, garrya is often used against a wall where it will build into a large, stately specimen. It comes from Oregon and California and, although reasonably hardy in most places, the warmth of a wall is welcome in cooler spots and encourages flowering.

type Shrub, evergreen

size Height and spread 2-3.5m (6-12ft), more in milder areas or with wall support

foliage Evergreen, dull matt green, leathery oval leaves with informally waved edges

flowers Catkins are best from the end of autumn to the end of winter. Plants are either male or female. The males have very much longer catkins, from 8-15cm (3-6in) long, but in milder weather and areas up to 20-30cm (8-12in) of silvery-grey and light green. Catkins are usually in pairs or clusters and are freely produced

site Except in cold areas shrubs can be grown in the open or against walls. Garrya is a particularly useful shrub near walls, as it can manage well in poor soils and is not the thirstiest of plants

care Plants grow quite quickly and need little attention. Some support may be welcome for the first season or so

propagation By layering low branches or by air layering in late summer

cultivars 'James Roof' is a selected male clone with long catkins

CORNUS MAS

CORNELIAN CHERRY
(Cornus mas)

The cornelian cherry is not really a cherry and its 'common' name is rarely used. It is a very hardy European species, although the small (2cm/¾in) fruits are rarely produced in cooler climates. The plant is very pretty in deep winter, with the bare stems enclosed in a misty yellow cloud of star-like flowers. When it reaches tree status it is very impressive.

type Shrub growing into small tree. Spreading and twiggy

size Height and spread 6m (20ft)

foliage Deciduous, leaves 5-10cm (2-4in) long by 2-4cm (¾-1½in) wide, matt dark green turning purple-red in autumn

flowers and fruit Tiny stars only 3mm (⅛in) across, but in rounded umbels about 2cm (¾in) diameter, crowded on the previous season's growth in mid- to late winter. Edible red 'cherry' fruits appear in late summer to autumn

site Flowering is best seen against a dark background (or silhouetted against blue winter skies)

soil Most

care Easy, blooms freely from being freshly planted until it becomes an old, substantial tree. Very hardy

propagation Layer a low branch, or try air layering in midsummer

PLANTS OF THE MONTH

The witch hazels carry their scented, spidery flowers in a range of colours, including:
Hamamelis mollis, gold
H.m. **'Pallida'**, primrose, very free flowering
H. × *intermedia* **'Arnold Promise'**, yellow
H. × *i.* **'Diane'**, red, leaves turn gold, orange and red in autumn
H. × *i.* **'Jelena'**, orange

BEAUTIFUL BERRIES
Many shrubs and trees continue to carry heavy crops of berries until late winter, in particular firethorns (Pyracantha), Cotoneaster symonsii and others, thorns such as Crataegus lavallei 'Carrierei' and Skimmia japonica.

practical project

REPLACING GRASS WITH GRAVEL

An area of trimmed green grass looks good, but it is not achieved without effort and cost. A small area can look mean, and demand far too much work to keep it looking well.

A realistic assessment of the costs listed in the margin will show that a lawn can be the most expensive part of the garden. It must be a matter of choice whether it is thought worth the expenditure.

There are alternatives, especially over relatively small areas where the laying down of gravel or other covers such as paving or shredded bark may have considerable economic advantages. Such hardwearing covers will need far less maintenance and allow you to spend more time with the plants. Another advantage of hard coverings is that they are less vulnerable to the vicissitudes of the weather – they are more efficient all-weather surfaces than grass. Droughts will not affect them much: gravel, for example, tends to provide a free-draining surface but also acts as a mulch to contain moisture below, and the contrast between plants and gravel can be very pleasing to the eye.

There may also be a case for planning a gravelled area close to the house while maintaining a lawn at some distance. This would make the transition from house to garden more gradual. Remember there must be a gap between the finished level of any work around the house and the damp course; 15cm (6in) is a sensible minimum to keep clear.

Gravel blends with brickwork and paving easily, and its colour can harmonise and contrast with other materials as well as the surrounding plant life. In fact, it is as a contrast to planted areas that gravel can be most effective, and there is no need to try to establish a firm line between gravel and border as there normally is with grassed areas.

For all their advantages, there is always the danger of using too many different types of material – gravel, bricks, paving, wood – in proximity and creating a jarring effect. It may be safer to use just two or three materials to aim for a sense of unity. However, if the use is graduated, such as a pathway of paving stones, perhaps imitation York stone, leading through a gravelled area and into a grassed one, this will provide a strong unifying feature and look very attractive.

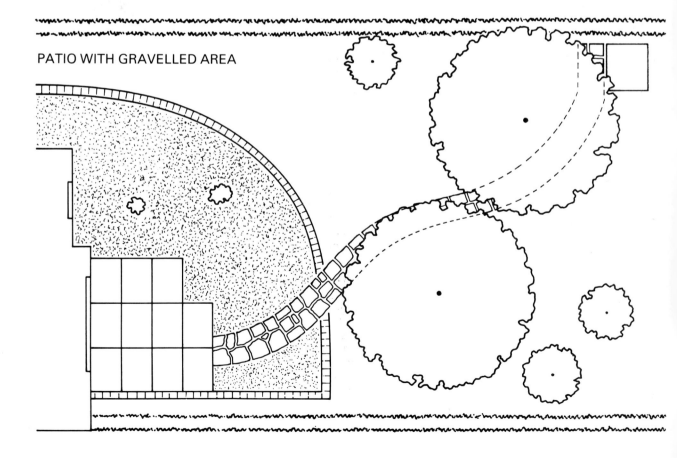

PATIO WITH GRAVELLED AREA

MAKING THE GRAVELLED AREA

■ Mark out the area to be gravelled.

■ Kill off all weeds, especially difficult perennials like nettles, docks and bindweed. Perennials are best destroyed by using a weedkiller containing glyphosate.

■ If converting a grassed area, remove the turf. (Stack the grass to rot down and for use in composts.)

■ Rake over and ensure that the area is well drained – you do not want a pond after each fall of rain.

■ On well-drained sites you can miss out the next two steps. Where there is a drainage problem (ie you find water lying in a trial hole some 60cm (24in) deep), field drains should be laid to a lower area or drain.

■ Where surface drainage is important, the soil can be excavated to a depth of 8-10cm (3-4in) and a 5-8cm (2-3in) layer of coarse gravel laid before the final 4cm (1½in) of fine gravel.

■ Where gravel is laid on top of soil, first lay some plastic sheeting as a membrane to prevent weed germination.

■ Introduce the gravel and spread it evenly to a depth of 8-10cm (3-4in). Using a fork, puncture the plastic sheeting to allow any surplus water to drain away.

■ If you intend to introduce plants within the gravelled area, clear the gravel from the planting spot and cut a cross in the plastic sheeting. Site the specimen and plant firmly, then tuck back the plastic and re-cover with gravel. A plastic-free zone should be allowed around the plant – a good measure to stick to is twice the diameter of the pot from which it was taken.

CHOICE OF GRAVEL

Choice of gravel type will depend on the surrounds. It may take the form of crushed and graded rock chips, granite chippings or pea gravel. Pea gravel always looks good, as the colours are a little varied. Granite can look rather dismal. Cotswold stone chippings are rather garish when first laid, but will tone down quickly and provide a good contrast to the plants.

> ## **T**IMESCALE
>
> ■ *The time required to complete this project will depend on the extent of the area involved, and whether or not soil has to be removed and drainage organised* ■

Iris pallida 'Variegata'

PLANTS TO GROW IN GRAVEL

Artemisia absinthium 'Lambrook Silver'
Brachyglottis (*Senecio*) 'Sunshine'
Convolvulus sabatius
Euphorbia characias
E. myrsinites
Iris pallida 'Variegata'
Dwarf conifers

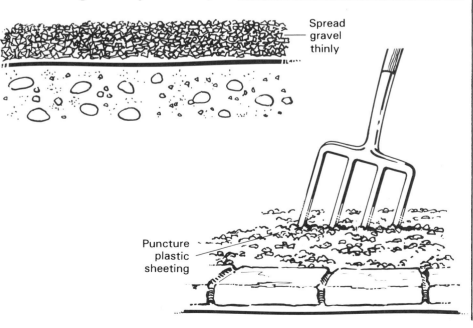

Spread gravel thinly

Puncture plastic sheeting

Convolvulus sabatius

FEBRUARY

This can seem like the lowest part of the year. There can be lovely days that seem almost to herald spring – but it is likely to be a false one. Best to enjoy the brightness whilst it lasts before this month gets back to its more sombre ways.

Many gardeners will think of this time as the beginning of their year. It is a busy month of sowing seed and getting everything ready for the coming new cycle of growth. By now it is possible to see some plants already committed to action. Bulbs are growing apace; hazels and willows are festooned with catkins; maybe the first forsythia buds are bursting.

And maybe the gardener has everything tidied up outside. Last year's debris has finally been cleared away, canes and other temporary supports are in store. It is a time to feel virtuous. The weeds have not really started to grow. There are no routine jobs that threaten peace of mind – and here perhaps is the point. Gardening is neither completely an art or wholly a science, it is more an attitude of mind. Perhaps we should settle for the word 'recreation' – a process that recreates our surroundings and ourselves.

This month we can spare a moment to be philosophical. Soon we shall be busy with our recreation and will be enacting out the truths of little catches such as 'a stitch in time . . .' or 'Never let a weed see Sunday'. Certainly jobs done now to counter possible weed growth later will be very worthwhile. The time of maximum slug activity is also approaching, and if we can keep this part of creation in some subjection now, our plants may cope themselves later.

tasks
FOR THE
month

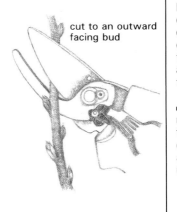

cut to an outward
facing bud

CHECKLIST

☐ Carry out winter pruning
☐ Sow seeds
☐ Put garden designs into practice – begin
construction work

WINTER PRUNING

If not already completed, any pruning required on fruit and decorative trees and shrubs is best finished before the sap becomes active. Garden lore is rich with advice, learned books are there to be consulted. However, most of us, and the plants in our charge, manage without degrees in 'prunology', and for ease and simplicity there are a few things it may help to remember.

■ Remove branches that reach from one side of the tree or shrub across the centre, those that chafe against others and ugly and unbalanced growths.

■ Always cut back close to a remaining bud and, if at all possible, choose a bud pointing outwards from the centre of the bush or tree.

■ With top fruit (trees such as apples and pears) try to allow plenty of air circulation around the branches.

■ For bush fruit like gooseberries you should be able to move a clenched fist around branches without getting lacerated.

■ Many decorative and fruit bushes flower and fruit on the previous year's wood. Pruning should therefore remove a good proportion of the flowering/fruiting wood after this harvest to encourage fresh wood for the following year.

Roses

Traditionalists make a lot of pruning bush (large-flowered) roses. Recent research has proved that bushes produce more blossom by being trimmed back by a third with shears or even a chain saw, which is far less time-consuming.

Species and old-fashioned roses require less pruning so, if this is not a task you enjoy, plant fewer of the bush varieties and more of these. Restrict yourself to removing obviously worn-out stems, ugly and diseased pieces and shoots that unbalance the form. Weak growth and bits that clutter the centre should also be removed.

SEED SOWING

Growing masses of bedding plants from seed is a lot of work and not recommended for the easy garden, but there will be some plants that you will enjoy raising and new ones you may want to try. If there is some heat available, this is a good month for sowing most seeds (look at the packet instructions, as some seeds need the action of frost to activate them). The warmth of the kitchen windowsill will be plenty to get most seeds germinating quickly: 18-21°C (65-70°F) is the range to which most seeds respond.

It is sensible to use seed compost free of organisms and weed seeds that could inhibit germination or damage or compete with fledgling seedlings. If you do not have a propagator, you can manage perfectly well with a seed tray or pot enclosed in a plastic bag to retain moisture and provide a mini eco-climate, or even a margarine tub covered with cling-film.

The 'rules' for successful seed raising are as follows:

RAMBLING AND CLIMBING ROSES

Remove weak and very old wood. Bring long growths lower and tie firmly – getting branches low and nearly horizontal encourages flowering and fresh growth from centre. Lowering strong branches may have to be done in stages, lowering, tying and then, some weeks later, repeating until reaching the final low position.

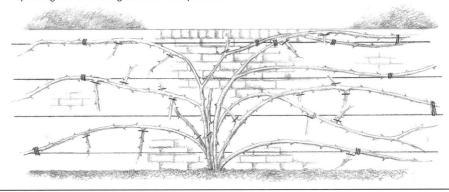

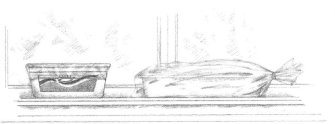

■ Use clean containers and fresh seed compost.

■ Sow seed thinly, so that germinating seedlings are not crowded and do not get drawn upwards seeking space and light.

■ Keep the compost moist but not sodden, which is best achieved in a sealed container or plastic bag.

■ Maintain warmth.

■ As soon as seed begins to germinate, allow in more air and make sure that the seedlings have full light.

■ Seed leaves (cotyledons) are followed by the first true leaf – one which begins to show the characteristics of the species. When the first true leaf is fully developed, the seedlings will be ready for pricking out into individual pots or spaced in trays.

■ Do not allow the growing seedlings to dry out, but do not drown them either.

■ Try to prick out only a few more seedlings than you need. There is a temptation to use all the seedlings, thinking in terms of 'waste not, want not', but time, effort and space spent raising surplus plants is wasted. Keep yourself under control.

PUTTING GARDEN DESIGNS INTO PRACTICE

This section is a plea to use commonsense, to think through larger jobs before starting and to plan how they may be put into effect with the minimum of effort and bother.

Large rocks and heavy paving stones can sometimes seem to have a life of their own once brought out of their resting state. Rely on the principle of levers to ease the movement of inert masses and try to avoid getting your feet and hands between two hard or heavy surfaces unless you have all under tight control.

> ### WARNING
>
> ■ *When laying paving slabs, try to keep your hands to the sides that are free to avoid obvious accidents between two close guillotine-type surfaces* ■

Steps to safe and easy construction

■ With any construction job, the materials to be used should be delivered as close to the working site as possible. Adequate space should be allowed for working – trying to manage in cramped quarters is likely to lead to accidents or at least to unnecessary body stress.

■ Some jobs may require two pairs of hands. Organise yourself so that you purchase, bribe, cajole or blackmail another pair of reliable hands for the planned time, and allow plenty of time for any job in order to avoid rushing and perhaps skimping on safety, and not finishing with as thorough a job as you would like. It follows from this that you should tackle important tasks when fresh, and not continue working when tired and more prone to error and misjudgement.

■ Good pathways and tools are important. Investigate local plant-hire firms if you need larger equipment like concrete-mixers, cultivators or even bigger sprayers. Any larger-scale excavation work can be put out to tender. If you do this, the specifications of the job need to be put on paper as precisely as possible and detailed written quotations obtained.

■ The installation of ponds, pergolas, screens and permanent pathways can be made easier by using prefabricated units. These will be much more expensive than raw materials but will save time and effort. Leave the installation of electrically operated pumps to start water flows or fountains to qualified experts.

■ A residual current device (earth-leakage circuit breaker) must be used between the mains supply and any machine using electricity. Any connection in power cables must be a properly manufactured waterproof one. If a connector is used, the female end should be at the electricity supply (live) end and the male with prongs be on the part leading to the machine. Cables must be fully unwound and left loose when being used; if a tightly wound cable carries electricity it will quickly warm up and soon become dangerous, perhaps even to the point of igniting.

OTHER JOBS

Prune *Clematis jackmanii* types to within 30cm (12in) of the base.

Check all supports for rotting. Replace rotten stakes. Treat all new stakes with wood preservative

Strong clumps of herbaceous plants can be lifted and split, and healthy outside pieces replanted

IN THE GREENHOUSE

Check overwintering plants such as geraniums (pelargoniums). Pot on any cuttings and plants that are ready

Prune fuchsias; cut back side shoots to the base and main branches to 25cm (9in)

Start seed sowing

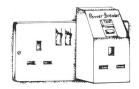

plants
OF THE
month

WINTER-FLOWERING HEATHER

Erica carnea varieties to try include:

'Ann Sparkes', reddish purple, leaves tipped yellow
'December Red', pinky-purple, dark blue-green foliage
'Eileen Porter', neat, good red
'King George', rich pink
'Springwood White', trailing plant
'Vivellii', deep carmine, black-green foliage, dwarf

WINTER-FLOWERING HEATHER
(Erica carnea)

A very hardy heather, with forms that start blooming in late autumn and last for months. Other cultivars continue until the spring is well advanced. This species is tolerant of lime in the soil and so is a plant for everyone. It makes excellent weed-inhibiting ground cover to the front of borders or shrubberies. (See on p116 for more detail and propagation methods.)

type	Hardy, spreading shrub
size	Height 8-30cm (3-12in), spread up to 1m (3ft)
foliage	Evergreen, narrow needlelike leaves, usually dark green but with cultivars that are yellow and others flushed red or purple
flowers	Range from pure white to pink, mauve and deep purple-red. Mid-autumn to mid-spring. (See margin)
planting	Plant young specimens quite deeply, 2.5cm (1in) or more deeper than in the pot. Planting can be done any time, perhaps early spring is the best
site	An open, sunny spot with reasonable drainage
care	Plants need little special care, but could be given a top dressing of grit and humus to aid fresh rooting, and when older can be given a light 'haircut' with shears immediately after blooming if needed to keep them tidy. This will also encourage fresh growth and flowering
cultivars	See margin

ERICA CARNEA CULTIVARS

HYBRID WINTER HEATHER
(Erica × darleyensis)

A series of very strong-growing heathers that will do well in poor soils, including limy ones. They will all start flowering in late autumn and go through to late spring, making excellent ground cover around shrubs.

type	Hardy, spreading shrub
size	Height 45cm-1m (18in-3ft), spread 1-1.5m (3-5ft)
foliage	Evergreen, rich green, needle-like leaves
flowers	White to purple-red. Late autumn to late spring
site	Sunny, open position
care	Vigorous on all soils. Clip dead flowerheads in late spring
cultivars	'Arthur Johnson', 15cm (6in) spikes of rosy pink; 'Darley Dale', very free, pink; 'George Rendall', rich pink, foliage tipped cream in spring; 'Ghost Hills', deep pink; 'Kramer's Rote', red; 'Silberschmelze', vivid white against dark foliage

SNOWDROP
(Galanthus nivalis)

The common snowdrop is as lovely as any. It is difficult to have too many. If planted in open, leafy soil that is reasonably moist, bulbs will increase very quickly and clumps can be lifted every other year to be split up and

replanted immediately. If you do not have a resident population, purchase plants 'in the green' just after flowering, or dry bulbs as early as possible in the autumn.

type	Bulb of the daffodil family
size	Height at flowering 10-15cm (4-6in)
foliage	Grey-green, like miniature daffodil leaves
flowers	White with green tips on the three inner segments
planting	Plant bulbs 10cm (4in) deep in late spring in the green, or early autumn as dry bulbs
site	Between shrubs, in borders or in grass. Rate of increase in grass will be slower
soil	Humus-rich, open soils will accelerate propagation
care	Top-dress with leafy matter in autumn
propagation	Split clumps just as the leaves are beginning to fail, usually in the late spring. This is considerably better than the often recommended 'straight after flowering'

FLOWERING QUINCE
(*Chaenomeles speciosa*)

These attractive, twiggy and sometimes spiky shrubs may be offering flowers from early winter through until the new leaves start unfurling in mid-spring. They are splendid against walls, which provide extra heat to ripen the wood and encourage flowering buds to form; the protection of the wall also prompts the dark stems to open some early blossom.

type	Hardy shrub
size	Height 1-2.5m (3-8ft), spread 3-5m (10-16ft)
foliage	Deciduous, polished, oval dark green leaves
flowers	Five-petalled, wide cups rather like apple blossom, usually with a golden boss of stamens
planting	Best planted in late autumn
site	Sunny, well-drained site. Not a gross feeder
care	On walls, pruning of side shoots after flowering to a couple of buds will encourage lots of new flowering wood
propagation	By layering. Leave for a year before severing when rooted
cultivars	See margin

GALANTHUS NIVALIS

QUINCES

Chaenomeles cultivars include:

C.speciosa **'Apple Blossom'**, pink and blush
C.s. **'Moerloosei'**, white and pale pink
C.s. **'Nivalis'**, white
C.s. **'Simonii'**, semi-double dark red. Dwarfer bush than most
C. × superba **'Crimson and Gold'**, free-flowering dark red with golden stamens
C. × s. **'Knap Hill Scarlet'**, strong orange-red
C. × s. **'Pink Lady'**, soft pink

CHAENOMELES 'KNAP HILL SCARLET'

practical project

PATIOS AND CONTAINERS

PATIOS

The patio is very much the transition point between house and garden, and provides a valuable rest area for the gardener. In good weather it becomes the outside room; at all times it provides hardstanding space and a linking area between house and garden. Normally it will be against the house, but there may be homes where it makes sense to build the outdoor room somewhat apart, perhaps to take advantage of better shelter and sunshine hours. French windows will usually open on to the patio area, but could give access to a path leading to it – there is little point to a patio if it is not easily reached.

A patio needs space for garden furniture and an easily maintained, hardwearing surface. A low wall framing at least part of the patio can make sense, emphasising its role of outside room and providing a resting place for the wine glass.

Construction

■ Mark out the site, kill off all weeds and remove the first few inches of valuable topsoil.

■ Level the main area of the patio, taking care to allow a slight slope away from the house to help take rain water away and make cleaning easier. Remember, you must maintain a gap at least as wide as two brick courses between the finished construction and the damp course. On some sites it may be possible or necessary to form a secondary lower level with step or steps between the two. Normally this secondary level will be the lesser of the two areas, perhaps in the ratio of 1:2 or 2:5.

■ In places where drainage is a considerab problem, excavate and then introduce a 10-15cm (4-6in) layer of rough hardcore, with drainage pipes to take away surplus water to a lower spot or drain.

■ Cover the levelled area with a polythene

TIMESCALE

■ *The time taken to complete a patio will depend on the extent of the project, your own energy/free time, and the amount of help you can get. There is no need to rush the job – taking it in stages may highlight the importance of certain features and even bring about some modification of the original plan. It is better to allow several weekends than to try to complete everything in one go* ■

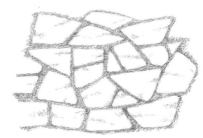

membrane to help prevent weed growth. The polythene can be lost under the sand which will be the base on which the patio slabs are to be laid. (For laying slabs see p45.)

■ York or imitation York flagstones look splendid and their varying sizes give a more natural feel than formal paving stones. However, there are now a variety of manufactured stones that should be considered before starting – larger garden centres and builders' merchants usually have sample areas laid out. Bricks can be used, or large blocks which look like bricks. These blocks will make the job much quicker to complete and can be a lot cheaper. Finally, there needs to be some sympathy between the patio materials and those of the house.

■ Where children are involved, the patio is probably best kept fairly simple in form, as it will be an important play area. Where adults only will use it, parts of the patio need not be slabbed over but can be left open or covered with chippings. Plants can be introduced into these areas. Make sure, though, that the slabbed sections are large enough to accommodate your garden furniture, as one of the primary functions of a patio is to provide an area for relaxation and contemplation of the rest of the garden.

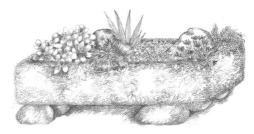

CONTAINERS

The patio is a stage. It can be kept clear and make its impact from the materials and perhaps surrounding walls, or 'decor' may be introduced. Garden furniture can be left more or less permanently in place. There may be one or two plants living in the patio space, perhaps climbers scrambling up supports and growing overhead pergola-wise. But the stage changes aspect as the months pass, and this is enhanced if planted containers are added to the patio.

Sometimes it is the container itself which makes the most impact. It can act as a piece of sculpture even if it is only a large earthenware pot, while a huddle of three or more pots can create a tableau – and there is no plant care involved! Only introduce artefacts that you really enjoy. After all, this is the part of the garden scene that is likely always to be under view, and individual taste will be the deciding factor.

The patio can be just the place to site a well-planted and attractive original or new 'antique' stone trough. With very little care these can look attractive all round the year.

NOTE

■ *Unless there is ample space and plenty of shelter within close flying distance, the patio will probably be too close to the house for a birdbath or table to be included* ■

plants
OF THE
month

Allium moly

OTHER SMALL BULBS WHICH LOOK AFTER THEMSELVES

Allium moly, golden garlic
Chionodoxa luciliae, glory-of-the-snow
Crocus species
Fritillaria meleagris, snakeshead fritillary
Galanthus species, snowdrops
Muscari azureum
Ornithogalum umbellatum, star of Bethlehem
Puschkinia scilloides
Scilla bifolia
S. mischtschenkoana
S. siberia

WINTER ACONITE
(Eranthis hyemalis)

This European species can naturalise itself to make a sheet of yellow in late winter. It will associate well with snowdrops and hellebores.

type	Small, knobbly tuber
size	Height at flowering 10-15cm (4-6in)
foliage	Bright green, deeply cut, rounded leaves and a ruff of leaf-like bracts in a circle under each buttercup flower
flowers	Upward-facing golden cups. Late winter
planting	Plant tubers about 5cm (2in) deep in a cool, moist spot. Best 'in the green' late spring, otherwise early autumn
site	Light woodland or between shrubs. 'Guinea Gold' can be given a choicer spot at the front of a bed or border or in the rock garden. It is obviously much more of a star than its yeoman parents and of course it cannot make a nusiance of itself as could the species, by seeding in every crevice
soil	Best in leafy, moist soil
care	No special requirements
propagation	Allow seed to fall and produce new plants. 'Guinea Gold' should be dug up a week or two after flowering and the tubers split and replanted
cultivars	There is a very similar Turkish species, *E.cilicica,* and a hybrid between the two called 'Guinea Gold', which is larger, bolder and stronger

BLUEBELL
(Hyacinthoides non-scripta English bluebell, *H.hispanica* Spanish bluebell)

English bluebell woods are a national treasure and rarer than normally believed. The British native *Hyacinthoides non-scripta* has arching flower stems with bells hanging from one side. The bolder Spanish *H. hispanica* has stouter, more open bells displayed all round a rigidly upright stem. The two species will hybridise. Both are strong, possibly invasive species but attractive with shrubs and trees as well as in rough grass. If you want the native kind make sure that bulbs have not been plundered from woods; normally you would tell this from their ungraded sizes. The profile below refers to *H. hispanica.*

type	Bulb
size	Height at flowering 30cm (12in)
foliage	Low, arching, strap-shaped, glossy leaves
flowers	Hanging bells of blue, a tone or two lighter than those of *Hyacinthoides non-scripta.* Mid- and late spring
site	With the above warning of its invasive nature in mind, this can nevertheless be recommended as a trouble-free bulb to grow between and below trees and shrubs and in rough grass
care	No special requirements
propagation	These bulbs produce large quantities of seed which grows freely if not hoed. Bulbs increase quickly to form clumps. To hasten the process, bulbs can be lifted and split as soon as the leaves die down
cultivars	There are good white forms and some pinks available

SMALL SPRING BULBS

Once planted, most of these small bulbs will appear year after year, increasing their numbers and decorative effect considerably. Most multiply steadily by bulb division, but also produce lots of seed that grows rapidly into flowering-sized bulbs.

ANEMONE
(Anemone nemerosa, A. blanda)

A. nemerosa is the British wild anemone. *A. blanda* is same size and just as easy.

type	*Anemone nemerosa:* narrow creeping rhizomes; *A. blanda:* dark, knobbly tubers
size	Height at flowering 10-20cm (4-8in)
foliage	Attractive three-lobed, deeply cut, mid-green erect leaves that disappear in late spring
flowers	*A. nemerosa* can form carpets of white nodding flowers flushed pink. There are double and blue forms. *A. blanda* opens with wide, many-petalled blooms of bright blue, white or pink
planting	Plant 2.5-4cm (1-1½in) deep
site	Well-drained spot in open or light shade, excellent between shrubs
soil	Open, leafy soils with good drainage
care	No special requirements
propagation	Divide rhizomes or tubers a few weeks after flowering and replant immediately
cultivars	See margin

ANEMONE BLANDA

WOOD ANEMONES

***Anemone nemerosa* cultivars to naturalise:**

'Alba Plena', double white
'Allenii', lavender blue
'Robinsoniana', lavender
'Wilk's White', large white

DUTCH CROCUSES

'Early Perfection', violet purple, early
'Enchantress', light purple with silvery gloss. Mid-season
'Flower Record', dark purple
'Large yellow'. Earlier than others
'Peter Pan', white
'Pickwick', white and purple stripes
'Queen of Blues', pale blue with lighter margins
'Vanguard', light blue, two weeks earlier than others so company for **'Large yellow'**

CROCUS

From autumn through to late spring there is a succession of crocus species in flower. In very early spring *Crocus tommasinianus* carries thin spires of pale mauve, followed by some of the more chubby *C. chrysanthus* and *C. biflorus* cultivars in white, creams, yellows, golds and oranges, as well as blues and mauves. Now the larger, fat Dutch crocuses open. One of these is *C.* 'Jeanne d'Arc', described in the profile below.

type	Corm
size	Height at flowering 5-10cm (2-4in)
foliage	Narrow, dark green spikes with a central silver-white stripe
flowers	Pure white with golden-orange stigmata. Midwinter to early spring
planting	Plant corms 5-10cm (2-4in) deep
site	Open, sunny spot. Can be grown light grass for years if the foliage is not cut too early
soil	Well drained
care	Try to allow the foliage to die down naturally
propagation	Lift corms when the foliage

CROCUS 'JEANNE D'ARC'

	becomes strawy, divide them up and replant immediately
cultivars	See margin

practical project

MAKING A COMPOST AREA

Composting reduces waste to valuable humus and also helps keep the garden tidy. Even a small garden can benefit.

For effective composting and ease of working, the aim is to construct an efficient unit that also looks neat. Where only small quantities are concerned, a simple, labour-saving choice would be to gather the rubbish in dustbin liners or similar bags and allow the rotting to take place within the bags. An alternative would be to purchase one of the many ready-made compost bins now on the market.

Organic material is rotted by the action of bacteria, and this process requires moisture, air and warmth. Of the manufactured bins, the larger ones (about 1m (3ft) cube, ie about 1cu m (30cu ft)) are likely to be more efficient than smaller ones, as there will be a greater proportion of the material in the centre where decomposition is more thorough. With large quantities of waste it will be best to make your own units as detailed below.

If you have only minimal quantities of waste, a bin of 0.3-0.4cu m (10-15cu ft) will suffice. Select a bin that provides aeration but is not so open that the compost is likely to dry out and lose heat. Some of the plastic ones are the easiest to manage and the tidiest. Ensure that the bin is easy to open and that rotted compost can be removed easily.

CONSTRUCTING YOUR OWN BINS

The measurements given here can be adjusted but it is unwise to make bins too small. In the following example, the aim is to construct two adjoining bins each as near as possible to a 1m (3ft) cube.

■ Mark out an area 2 × 1m (6 × 3ft) on the chosen site.

■ Concrete six 10cm (4in) – or good-quality 8cm (3in) – square posts into the ground to a depth of approximately 38cm (15in), leaving 1m (3ft) above ground level. One post will mark each corner of the rectangle, the remaining two dividing the long sides into halves.

■ The back and sides of the bins are made by nailing on slats measuring approximately 8 × 2.5cm (3 × 1in), allowing air gaps of 4-5cm (1½-2in) between them.

■ The fronts are made as a removable section of the same slats nailed to uprights the height of the bin. Nail upright slats to the insides of

MATERIALS TO COMPOST

Garden weeds
Fallen leaves
Grass cuttings mixed with other materials
Less woody shredded garden prunings
Vegetable waste from the kitchen

The more diverse the mix the better. The addition of a scatter of soil will introduce bacteria. Sulphate of ammonia will add nitrogen to encourage quick rotting. This is cheap and as effective as brand-name rotting agents

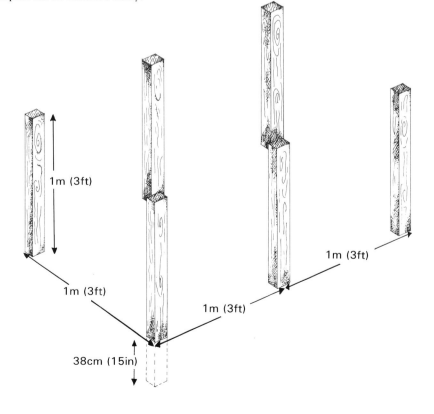

1m (3ft)

1m (3ft)

1m (3ft)

1m (3ft)

38cm (15in)

the open ends of the bins so that the moveable fronts can be slotted down easily and as easily removed.

■ A lid or cover over the top (even old carpet will do) will retain useful heat.

The advantage of having two bins is that the contents of one can be turned into the other when compost-making is proceeding rapidly, mixing the less rotted material from the top and outsides with the well-rotted material from the centre of the heap. Alternatively, it allows one binful to be maturing whilst leaving the other for fresh material.

Air can be encouraged into the base using either an initial layer of rough, bulky material like brassica stalks, or wooden supports or rows of bricks.

HOW COMPOSTING WORKS

■ *There are two series of bacteria whose mission in life is to break down organic material into humus: the* aerobic *organisms that work in the presence of oxygen, and the* anaerobic *ones that manage without. A heap starting as an energetic, aerobic, heat-producing, fast-burning/rotting heap can reduce vegetable matter to compost in a matter of eight weeks, but it may end up as an anaerobic, slow mover. The advantage of the aerobic fast-burn is that the heat generated – around 65°C (150°F) in the centre – will be ample to kill weed seeds, pests and most diseases* ■

RULES FOR COMPOSTING

■ **Bins with open bases should be placed on the soil, not on paving or concrete**

■ **Site the compost area out of sunshine and strong winds**

■ **Keep compost materials moist but not wet**

 When adding very dry material to the bin, moisten it first

The back and sides are made with slats of 8 x 2.5cm (3x1in) nailed to the uprights. The fronts (*right*) are made in the same way but are attached to separate uprights so that they can be removed.

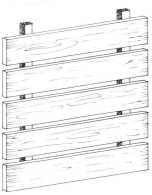

MARCH

Often a month of contrasts, one day winter and the next glorious
spring, by its end the energy of the new season will be fully
apparent. Explosive masses of golden forsythias reach towards the
pink clouds created by almonds and the wonderful Prunus
cerasifera *cultivars, every dark stem wreathed with a mass of
blossom in white, pink or red. Closer to the ground, the little
alpine plants are celebrating the end of winter and have burst into
their frenetic activity, blossom and then leaves aiming to complete
their tasks before the winter closes in again.*
*Slugs are on their slimy march and the first insects are getting busy
– some days the heathers are already alive with bees. The grass, if
we have any, can no longer be ignored, and the mower will have
to be brought out again – will it start first time?*
*Hazels and some willows may be losing the freshness of their
catkined glory. There are other, smaller willows waiting to break
open their buds and in the shrubbery the lovely soft yellow catkins
of* Corylopsis pauciflora *and* C. spicata *may now be at their
best, although they were already well in evidence last month.
Shrubs and trees that are not yet in bloom are fattening in bud
and can hardly wait. Some that we do not really regard as first-
line floral beauties surprise us again: the maples are pretty with
bright orange and red bracts with limy-coloured anthers.
Conifers, too, can delight. The dwarf* Pinus mugo *forms have
their new foliage ready orange-wrapped and looking like festive
candles all over their otherwise solemn grey greenery. Some
energetic shrubs are unwrapping their leaves to make stem and
leaf patterns.*
*And the daffodils come dancing to the front of the stage. They have
arrived; spring must be here.*

tasks
FOR THE
month

CHECKLIST

- Begin using fertiliser as necessary
- Plant lily bulbs and herbaceous plants; finish planting bare-rooted trees and shrubs as soon as possible
- Carry out the first grass cut of the season
- Begin a programme of slug and pest control
- Pruning summer-flowering shrubs

MAKING THE MOST OF FERTILISERS

All creation is on the move and needs feeding, but gardeners should be selective in their choice and use of fertilisers to avoid wasting both time and money.

There is a natural breakdown of organic matter that will release nutrients to dissolve in the soil water and be passed up from the rooting system to the factory floor of the leaves. The big three elements needed to work with carbon from the air are:

- *Nitrogen (N)* Essential for tissue building, especially leaves
- *Phosphorus (P)* Helps root growth, particularly when they are young. Helps ripening of fruits and seed production
- *Potassium (K)* Vital for photosynthesis processes in the leaves and laying down starches. Important for fruiting and aids disease resistance

Shrubs and trees are likely to find plenty of their own nutrients in the soil. You can help by giving mulches of leaves or manures. Well-made compost will provide a wide range of nutrients, while fresh bonfire ash will be rich in potash (potassium).

Most garden soils have enough nutrients in them to keep plants growing healthily. Only if you are anxious to give an extra boost will it be worth augmenting this with a balanced 'artificial' fertiliser. Bagged fertilisers come as pure chemicals such as sulphate of potash, or organic ones such as bonemeal. Standard kinds on sale will give their chemical analysis for the three main elements, NPK (see panel).

Recommended rates of application should not be exceeded.

As a rule, organic fertilisers release their nutrients slowly, inorganic ones much more rapidly. Potassium salts are particularly soluble and so it is sensible to give several small doses rather than one large one.

Very direct feeding can be achieved by spraying foliar feed on to any plants that you feel need extra help. Make sure that the sprayer is completely clean of any other spray, perhaps weedkiller, before starting. Prudent gardeners who spray a lot are likely to keep two sprayers, one for killing agents and the other for feeding and protective chemicals.

Do not waste time and money on fertilisers unless they are needed. Many established gardens may not need any extra unnatural fertiliser boost: often soils can be overloaded with phosphorus and even potash if continually treated. Nitrogen supplies may need augmenting, but avoid heavy doses of sulphate of ammonia. Two or three very light dustings at intervals will be safer and more effective, and slow-release kinds would be advisable in high-rainfall areas. Poor soils can be given a fillip by an annual scatter this month of a general fertiliser. Always try to avoid splashing concentrated fertilisers onto the leaves or stems of plants.

PLANTING

This is likely to be the last 'best' month when bare-rooted shrubs and trees can be planted. Often well-rooted specimens can be bought at this time at bargain prices. They are only a bargain,

CHEMICAL COMPOSITION OF FERTILISERS

ORGANIC
- Bonemeal: 8-22%P, 4%N, slow acting
- Steamed bonemeal: 25-30%P, 1%N, slow acting
- Hoof and horn: 13%N, slow acting
- Fish, blood and bone: 5N. 6P. 5K
- Dried blood: 12-14%N, quick-release nitrogen

INORGANIC
- Sulphate of ammonia: 21%N, quick-release nitrogen fertiliser, makes soil a little more acidic
- Nitrate of soda: 16%N, quick acting, unsuitable for heavy soils
- Superphosphate: 18%P, quick acting
Triple superphosphate: 46%P, quick acting but longer lasting
- Potassium nitrate: 38%K, quick acting, expensive
- Sulphate of potash: 40%K, quick acting

Mixed fertilisers are offered under 'trade' names. In Britain three leading ones are:
- National Growmore: 7N. 7P. 7K, reliable general fertiliser
- Vitax 101: 26N. 0P. 26K, useful general fertiliser without phosphate, which is generally plentiful in soils
- Phostrogen: 10N. 10P. 27K, good general fertiliser

however, if you can make good use of them, planting them immediately in a good site and keeping them moist for the weeks and months ahead.

This is an ideal time for introducing many herbaceous plants into the garden, while some that may not have got established very well in the late autumn will be raring to go. Large potted specimens which can be purchased now and safely split and planted this month include Michaelmas daisies and other asters, achilleas, veronicas, hostas, scabious, macleayas, monardas, ligularias and campanulas (see p101 for details).

Bulbs that can be planted this month could include lilies, especially the easy Asiatic hybrids. Expect to leave these to grow and flower for two or three years before lifting and dividing (see p78).

CUTTING THE GRASS

The first grass cut of the season should be a light one, so set the mower blades high. In the easy garden, if you have grass to be cut it is best not to try to get the level down to bowling-green near-baldness: that way lies the danger of brown deserts in periods of drought and more and more work. It is best to retain about 4-5cm (1½-2in) of growth. This may mean mowing fairly frequently during the growing period, perhaps once every week or ten days – or more frequently according to your personal degree of lawn-worship. Try to wean yourself off the delight of seeing stripes of freshly cut grass, unless you particularly enjoy the mild exercise of following the mower.

The most tedious part of lawn mowing is probably the disposal of cut grass. If you

are harvesting this for compost-making, try to mix it with other material so that you do not clog up the heap with massive doses of pure grass. It is a very good idea to save plastic bin bags of other material to use for mixing in periods of rapid grass growth. Another useful way of getting rid of grass cuttings is to distribute them thinly between and below shrubs so they act as a mulch. Take care not to form such a deep layer that it becomes a thatch which mats together to turn away rainfall.

Alternatively, you could invest in a mower that cuts the grass so finely and leaves it so evenly distributed on the ground that the residue is quietly assimilated into the top turf. To manage this successfully the grass needs frequent cutting, so that any one cut provides only a manageable amount. This system might possibly encourage moss, but you may be happy to see moss in the lawn – and why not? It is pleasant to walk on and is, after all, green.

COMPLETE PRUNING OF SUMMER-FLOWERING SHRUBS

If in doubt, don't. However, there are some summer-flowering shrubs that will bloom very much better if cut back in early spring before new growth has started; the aim is to remove weak growth and much of last year's flowering wood. Those that benefit most include *Buddleja davidii* in all its colour forms, *Caryopteris* × *clandonensis* and *Spiraea japonica* in its many forms. An annual cutting of perhaps 10% of stems of *Spiraea* hybrids, *S.* 'Arguta' and *S.* × 'Vanhouttei' will help to keep them among the top performers.

SLUG AND PEST CONTROL

Slugs become very active in early spring. There are approximately thirty different species of slug, but relatively few are a real threat. They are led by the smallish field slug (*Deroceras reticulatum*), a grey or pale brown pest often with some spotting. The garden slug (*Arion hortensis*) is about 4cm (1½in) long and comes in greys and browns with a golden-orange underside.

Prevention being better than cure, especially in the easy garden, it is wise to tackle slug threats early and to be ready to deal with aphids before they build up. Leaving soil rough-dug in winter can expose pests and their eggs to attack from bird predators, to the cold and, more importantly, to wet. Pirimicarb will kill aphids whilst not being generally harmful to beneficial insects. Systemic insecticides protect individual plants and deal with specific attacks.

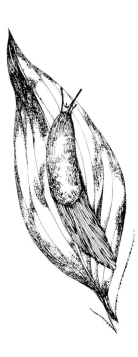

ESSENTIAL ELEMENTS IN PLANT NUTRITION

Carbon
Nitrogen
Potassium
Phosphorus
Hydrogen
Oxygen
Calcium
Sulphur
Magnesium
Iron
Boron   trace
Manganese   elements
Zinc

TACKLING SLUGS

An average of 25-40 slugs per square metre (yard) can be normal, so complete extermination is impossible. The following methods should help keep the damage they do to an acceptable level:

Slugs need moist conditions, so hoed, dried surfaces will help keep them in check.

Removing decaying waste, stones, waste wood, pots and trays will reduce the number of slug homes.

Deploying orange and apple peel and materials such as wet newspaper around the garden and then collecting the sheltering slugs frequently will help reduce numbers – slugs and snails are more active in the evening and at night and are best collected in the early morning.

Slug pellets distributed thinly on moist soil every ten days will go a long way towards controlling the population.

It is now, when new growth is being made and young plants introduced, that slugs can be the greatest problem, so action taken at this time will prevent major losses and save time and work later on.

plants
OF THE
month

SPIRAEA JAPONICA 'GOLDFLAME'

SPRING SHRUBS

From this month on most shrubs are moving through their gears, some getting into top performance quickly, such as the forsythias. Some, like the quinces (Chaenomeles) have been parading their blossom for several months, but now they give a final floral burst before donning leafy dress. Others have been respectably evergreen through the winter and now greet the spring with garlands; Berberis darwinii and B. × stenophylla are notable examples, as are the aristocratic camellias. The viburnum and weigela are listed here though they bloom some two months later.

VIBURNUM TOMENTOSUM

type	Hardy, deciduous shrub with spreading horizontal branches arranged in layers
size	Height 2m (6ft), spread 3m (10ft)
foliage	Light green, gently serrated leaves 5-10cm (2-4in) long and half as wide
flowers	Many flat umbels of white lace-cap flowers arranged along the branches from late spring into summer
site	Open, sunny spot
care	An easy shrub in normal drained soil
propagation	By layering

SPIRAEA JAPONICA 'GOLDFLAME'

Some of the spiraeas are among the most wonderful of flowering shrubs in the spring and early summer, but 'Goldflame' is a top-rank foliage plant.

type	Hardy, deciduous shrub, with compact masses of thin, upright and arching stems
size	Height and spread 75cm-1m (30in-3ft)
foliage	An outstanding foliage plant, especially attractive in spring and early summer. Young foliage is a glowing orange-red; this fades to gold and eventually a yellowish green
flowers	Each shoot ends with packed umbels of many small flowers of deep pink bordering red. Blooms from summer to autumn
site	Better in an open site
soil	Most
care	Needs little attention, but older specimens should have a proportion of older wood removed to encourage fresh growth, foliage and generous flowering
propagation	By softwood cuttings in summer
other cultivars	S. 'Arguta', deciduous, prolific white blossom later in spring, 1m (3ft); S. × 'Vanhouttei', deciduous, abundant white blossom, mid-spring, 2-3m (6-10ft)

 *WEIGELA* 'BRISTOL RUBY'

Weigelas are among the easiest of shrubs to grow quickly into flowering specimens. They respond well to pruning, so old plants can be cut back severely and renovated.

type	Hardy, deciduous, hybrid shrub. Rapid grower with upright and spreading stems
size	Height 2.5m (8ft), spread 2m (6ft)
foliage	Oval, serrated, rich green leaves
flowers	A mass of very dark buds opening to deep red trumpets through late spring and summer. Starts flowering freely as a young bush
site	Grows well on most soils and situations, in an open position or semi-shade
care	Very hardy and one of the easiest of all shrubs. Keep lively by pruning out old and straggling branches
propagation	By softwood cuttings taken in summer
other cultivars	'Candida' has white flowers; 'Eva Rathke' is an erect shrub with dark-budded crimson flowers; 'Variegata' has pink flowers and leaves with broad creamy-white margins

WEIGELA 'BRISTOL RUBY'

RHODODENDRON WILLIAMSIANUM

The thousands of different rhododendrons, ranging from tiny little hummocks to large trees, are regarded by many as the aristocrats of flowering shrubs. This is certainly an enthralling genus, often captivating gardeners with a limy soil who can only grow rhododendrons in containers or rather elaborate raised beds of peaty, leafy soil. If you have limy soil and love rhododendrons, better to be strong-minded and turn away, or move house.

type	Dense, spreading evergreen shrub
size	Height and spread 2m (6ft)
foliage	Young leaves an attractive shining bronze. Adult leaves a rich mid-green. Tidy oval shape
flowers	Crowds itself with loose sprays of wide bell flowers, reddish-pink in bud but rosy-pink when open. One of the most delightful of a fascinating genus for weeks in spring
site	Given the correct soil it is very hardy and resilient
soil	Like all rhododendrons, needs a neutral or acid soil
care	Grows very tidily and normally needs no care at all, although it will welcome annual mulches of leaf mould or other forms of humus
propagation	By layering
other cultivars	See margin

RECOMMENDED SPRING-FLOWERING SHRUBS

The following is a selection of generally easy, reliable shrubs, with flowers in a range of colours * marks those normally in bloom this month:

Berberis darwinii*, evergreen, golden-orange
Berberis × stenophylla*, evergreen, orange
Camellia × williamsii 'Donation'*, evergreen, rich pink
Ceanothus 'A. T. Johnson', evergreen, blue
Chaenomeles, Deciduous, red, orange, pink, white
Cytisus × praecox 'Allgold', evergreen effect, gold
Daphne × burkwoodii 'Somerset', deciduous, pink
Erica arborea alpina*, evergreen, white
Forsythia × intermedia 'Lynwood'*, deciduous, yellow
Genista hispanica, evergreen effect, golden
G. lydia, evergreen effect, golden
Halesia carolina (snowdrop tree), deciduous, white
Magnolia stellata*, deciduous, white
Osmanthus delavayi, evergreen, white
Pieris formosa forrestii, evergreen, white and pink cultivars
P. japonica, evergreen, white, mauve and pink cultivars
Prunus triloba, deciduous pink
Rhododendron, evergreen, whites, creams, yellows, pinks, mauves, reds
Ribes sanguineum, deciduous, pink
Salix lanata, deciduous, golden male flowers
Ulex europaeus 'Plenus', evergreen effect, golden
(See also Appendix 2)

practical project

PLANTING TREES

fastigiate

TREES IN SMALLER GARDENS

Trees are marvellous things. In the garden they help to ensure that all is not too two-dimensional: they pull the sky into the picture frame. They provide a strong presence and, if chosen carefully, plenty of interest in return for minimal maintenance.

Having said this, there are plenty of trees that it would be unkind or foolish to plant in the small garden. The place for a forest tree is in a forest; nor do we want to place in a prominent spot a tree that is continually dropping twigs and leaves, such as the otherwise engaging corkscrew willow, *Salix babylonica* 'Tortuosa'. Some trees exude juices that can annoy and disfigure what is below; others, whilst a joy for a brief period, like the flowering almonds, are almost boring for the rest of the year.

When space is limited you need to make a good choice. You will want a tree that makes a good shape, is not too large, looks well in leaf and perhaps has two seasons of special attraction, maybe spring blossom and autumn colour or fruit. The shape of the tree may well be the most important factor and, bearing this in mind, you may be able to select the 'fastigiate' (upright and narrow) form of a tree that would otherwise be totally unsuitable, such as beech or the tulip tree. Choice is also more difficult if you are restricted to a single tree. Is it to be a deciduous one with its changing interest through the seasons, or an evergreen that provides rather more staid colour but manages this throughout the year?

Bare-rooted versus container-grown

Some trees are offered as bare-rooted field-grown specimens rather than containerised. Planted in the late autumn or early winter, bare-rooted trees can get away well in the spring and soon overtake what one would think to be the container specimen's advantage of an established and almost undisturbed root system. If a tree has been too long in a pot the roots can become pot-bound and take a while to adventure into the surrounding soil and start making strong headway. The bare-rooted ones will certainly be substantially cheaper.

Site and spacing

Trees grow, and they need to be given room. They need placing where they are not going to require serious surgery in a few years' time, when branches threaten windows or spread alarmingly over into neighbour's airspace. If planted to screen an unsightly building or eyesore, it may be more effective to site the tree to the side of the object to lead the eye from it, rather than try to block it out completely. If more than one tree is to be planted they are often best positioned at different distances from the viewpoint so that the eye is taken from one to the other rather than being confronted by two sentries.

Planting

It is worth taking time and trouble at the beginning to plant your tree carefully and with attention to detail. This is a one-off job which will be repaid handsomely by a healthy, flourishing tree requiring little or no maintenance over the many years of its life.

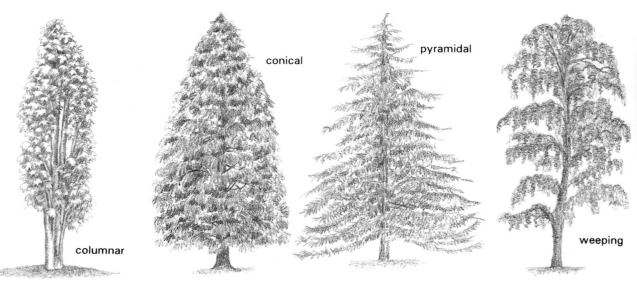

columnar

conical

pyramidal

weeping

■ Dig the soil deeply, to at least 30cm (1ft), excavate it and dig over the bottom of the hole to a depth of approximately 15cm (6in). A hole over a metre (yard) wide will be needed.

■ Hammer in a tree stake so that it protrudes 20-30cm (8-12in) above soil level; this will be used to secure the tree and prevent it rocking its rootstock loose in the wind.

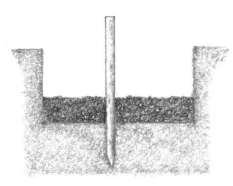

■ Mix compost, manure or other humus with the excavated soil. Place the tree in the hole to the same depth as it was planted on the nursery or in its container, or perhaps 25cm (1in) or so

deeper to allow for soil settlement. Replace the soil, making sure it is worked well down among the roots. There is little advantage in adding fertiliser at this stage. In very poor soils a sprinkle of superphosphate may aid rooting.

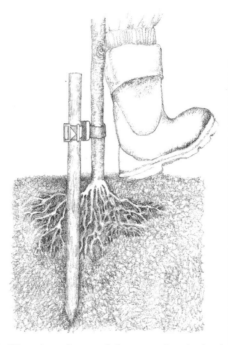

■ Firm the soil around the tree using the heel of your boot. Tie the tree to its stake using a proprietary tree tie.

After thoroughly watering the tree in, the best you can do while it is getting established is to make sure that it does not suffer from drought, keeping it well clear of weed growth and perhaps giving it an occasional mulching.

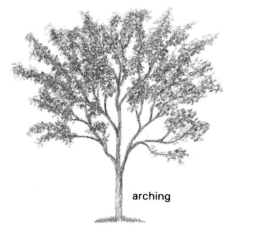

arching

contorted

RECOMMENDED EVERGREENS

Arbutus unedo
A. × *andrachnoides*
Chamaecyparis lawsoniana
C.l. 'Columnaris Glauca'
C.l. 'Lane'
Cornus capitata (in milder districts)
Eucalyptus nicholii
E. niphophila
Ilex aquifolium 'Argentea Marginata'
I.a. 'Golden Queen'
I.a. 'Golden Van Tol'
I.a. 'Silver Queen'
Juniperus scopulorum 'Skyrocket'
Taxus baccata 'Fastigiata', Irish yew
(See also Appendix 1)

RECOMMENDED DECIDUOUS TREES

Acer palmatum, Japanese maple
A. pseudoplatanus
'Brilliantissimum'
Betula ermanii
B. utilis, var. *jacquemontii* and other birches
Fagus sylvatica 'Dawyck', fastigiate beech
F.s. 'Dawyck Purple', fastigiate copper beech
Ginkgo biloba, maidenhair tree
Halesia carolina, snowdrop tree
Laburnum × *vossii*
Malus 'Lemoinei' and other crab apples
Morus nigra, mulberry
Prunus subhirtella 'Autumnalis', winter-flowering cherry
P . 'Kikushidare-zakura' and other flowering cherries
Pyrus salicifolia, willow-leaved pear
Sorbus vilmorinii and other sorbus
(See also Appendix 1)

APRIL

The poet thought this 'the cruellest month'. Perhaps he was having a bad day – for the gardener this is one of the most exciting times of year. Each day new plants burst into leaf and bloom, and it is all happening: birds are nesting, bees are busy and the market stall and garden centre are full of seedling plants.

Bulbs lead the rush to colour, shrubs and trees follow, and close to the ground a thousand different little alpine plants shake off thoughts of snow-capped mountain tops and produce their perfect flowers. Pots and trays of seedlings are growing strongly, and the grass is growing well and has taken on rich tones. Everywhere the unfurling foliage delights, and the fresh green touches in the hedges suddenly flood over all.

Many of our shrubs are as lovely in their new foliage as in bloom. Pieris *cultivars* are now opening their orange and red, shining young buds and leaves. Downy buds burst open on dark-stemmed whitebeam, Sorbus aria, *to become for a while a cloud of silver-white candles caught in the most elaborate of candelabra. All the maples are a joy, with the bright bracts of their expanding buds, their often limy flowers and gorgeously coloured young foliage.

In rougher grass, crowds of daffodils arrange their annual pageant, cultivars that can be left for decades without attention. What an investment!

Work may beckon, but if we are sensible this can be kept to a minimum. Some gardeners enjoy keeping great lengths of hedge in parade-ground order; for those taking the easy approach, a more informal screen of shrubs could do the same border duty, look highly decorative for most of the year and need little more attention than a passing 'thank you'.

The sun in shining, let us get into the garden.

tasks
FOR THE
month

C H E C K L I S T

☐ Plant out container-grown shrubs and perennials
☐ Begin sowing seeds outside
☐ Tidy up the rock garden
☐ Lay turf for a new lawn
☐ Begin a programme of weed control
☐ Propagate snowdrops and winter aconites

Calendula

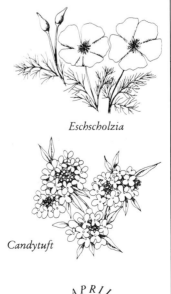

Eschscholzia

Candytuft

PLANTING

With the soil warming up and plenty of moisture about, most plants now become very active at root level. New plants will make quick new root growth, with the many tiny hair roots getting to work immediately to take up liquid nourishment.

Shrubs

Newly purchased shrubs, the backbone of the easy garden, can be planted now and will soon establish themselves. Pick healthy-looking specimens that are not pot-bound. Shrubs that have been living a long time in pots and have been cut back once or even twice are not likely to be good buys.

Plant firmly so that the base of the shrub ends up at the same level as it was in the pot, or just 2-5cm (1in) or so lower to allow for soil settling. If the soil is well

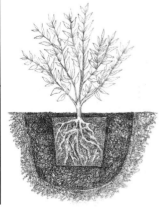

worked and given some extra humus there is normally no need to provide the fledgling shrub with any extra feed. Just make sure that the soil does not dry out and that weeds do not take hold.

Perennials

Herbaceous plants bought in containers may be planted as received or, if large, can be carefully divided to make more plants for the garden using two forks plunged back to back through the middle of the clump and then eased apart. With plants like hellebores, which dislike such brutal treatment, try more careful surgery. These can be washed free of soil and a sharp knife used to divide off pieces with generous amounts of root attached. The divisions can either be potted up in all-purpose compost and grown on for some weeks before planting out, or immediately planted out firmly in well-worked soil and kept moist. Unless they are freshly propagated stock, most herbaceous plants will benefit from being planted a touch deeper than when growing in containers.

SOWING SEED OUTSIDE

For summer colour, seed of flowering annuals can be broadcast in the sites where you have gaps to fill. Such

positions could include places in the border where clumps of daffodils and tulips are flowering now. A scatter of seed worked into the top of the soil can result in plants that will perform well later with almost no effort from the gardener. The easiest annuals to treat in this rather cavalier way include calendulas, candytuft, love-in-the-mist and eschscholzia. These will bloom and then drop their seed to stake a permanent claim to the territory. Self-sown seedlings should then apear in the autumn or spring; all you have to do is thin them out.

In the rock garden

It is sensible to check over rockery beds or gardens before the spring is too far advanced, so that small germinating weeds are dealt with before they get a strong roothold. This will save a lot of work later on. Whilst doing this job you may find series of seedlings from established rock plants, and some of these can be carefully removed and potted up for use elsewhere. The distribution and the young leaves of these seedlings will normally distinguish the good-guy plant seedlings from the bad-guy weeds.

Early in the month it is worth scattering some more gravel or chippings where the layer seems thin, especially in rock crevices. Whilst most rock plants will manage nicely with normal diets and even starvation regimes, some leading alpine growers admit to giving their plants a very light annual dusting of bonemeal or general fertiliser.

LAYING TURF:
SIX SIMPLE STEPS TO SUCCESS

If you want a quick lawn or grassed area, laying turf in

early spring may be the answer. Try to purchase weed-free turf from a reliable source.

- Ensure that the ground is level.

- Lay the turf on damp soil.

Make sure that the edges of the turves are butted together tightly.

- Brush over a light top dressing of sieved soil and compost.

Until the turf is established do not cut it too closely – maintain at least 4-5cm (1½-2in) of grass.

- Do not attempt to lay turf too late in the season, when drought conditions may make the project vulnerable. It is better to wait until early autumn (see p10´).

WEED CONTROL MADE EASY

Some people enjoy weeding, but there must be more fulfilling things to do. By weeding early and maintaining a regime, much can be done to reduce this work to the very minimum.

- Do not let weeds reach seeding stage. Grounsel, chickweed and bittercress get to flower and seed very quickly. Seed of most common weeds will remain viable in the soil only a few seasons not like that of poppies which can still germinate after 80 years!

- Ground-covering plants will help to inhibit weed germination. Trees, shrubs and spreading herbaceous plants of various kinds can all fall into this category.

- Hoeing the soil early will disturb germinating weeds and destroy them. The drier

hoed surface will prevent some seed from even starting into life.

- Mulches of well-made compost or shredded bark will go a long way to smothering incipient seedling weed growth. A 10cm (4in) layer of bark will normally last three seasons.

- Chemical sprays can be effective if carefully controlled and not allowed to drift on to legitimate plants. Spray only in still air conditions; direct the spray carefully at the weeds and follow the maker's instructions exactly.

- A small hand-held sprayer with an adjustable nozzle is very useful for spot weeding – it is possible to clear pernicious weeds like bindweed in one season from a very badly overgrown shrub border using such a sprayer.

- For deep-rooted perennial weeds such as docks, thistles and dandelions use a systematic weedkiller containing glyphosate.

REPLANTING SNOWDROPS AND WINTER ACONITES

By the end of this month or certainly the beginning of next the snowdrops and winter aconites will be getting a little tired in their foliage. This is the ideal time to lift and divide these easy bulbs and rhizomes and replant immediately, far better than just after flowering or in the autumn.

Snowdrops have small bulbs like daffodils and can be divided in the same way, but in open leafy soil they will also produce fresh bulbs from stolons – fleshy underground stems growing from established bulbs. These extra bulbs will be found below the level of the original bulbs, and by lifting and splitting them off every two or three years large numbers of snowdrops can be propagated.

The rootstock of a winter aconite is a knobbly rhizome which will snap easily into pieces. This should be done so that each piece has a growing point on it; then replant immediately.

LAWN WEEDS
The best time to kill lawn weeds with chemicals is when both grass and weeds are growing strongly; mid-spring is such a time. Apply a selective hormone weedkiller and follow the directions carefully – do not apply any more or any less than recommended.

TENDER PLANTS AND SWEET PEAS
By the end of the month, in warmer areas it may be possible to plant out overwintered tender plants such as geraniums (pelargoniums) or at least start hardening them off ready for planting soon. Sweet peas raised in an unheated greenhouse or frame may be planted out in their permanent quarters.

snap

plants
OF THE
month

DAFFODILS

From the evidence of various polls and the number that are sold each year, daffodils (Narcissus) are the most popular of all ornamental garden plants. It is little wonder: they represent the first main flower of spring – the winter is over; they are amongst the least demanding of plants and the easy garden can be full of kinds that, once planted, can be left for ever without lifting. In grass, rough ground and between shrubs, the bulbs will flourish with very little or no attention for decades. (See also p104).

In the border daffodil bulbs grow strongly and may need lifting every three or four years to split up the large clumps. If allowed to get overcrowded they will be fighting for food and light and will begin to be more leafy than flowery.

NARCISSUS CYCLAMINEUS 'BARTLEY'

The *N. cyclamineus* hybrids (see margin) are ideal for the easy garden: they come early, bloom freely, last for weeks in flower and the

NARCISSUS 'BARTLEY'

bulbs are healthy and increase quickly. They are ideal for naturalising, the foliage dying down early.

type	Hardy bulb
size	Height at flowering 25-35cm (10-14in)
foliage	Dies down early
flowers	Very persistent, rich gold with good stems. Early spring or even late winter
planting	Plant in early autumn with at least 10-15cm (4-6in) of soil over top of bulbs
site	In grass, between shrubs, in border
soil	Reasonably well drained
care	Will last for decades in the same site with minimal attention
propagation	See panel
other cultivars	See margin

WILD DAFFODIL
(*Narcissus pseudonarcissus*)

The wild daffodil. The bulbs do not like disturbance. The first year after planting they can look poor, with few flowers. Thereafter they get better and better year by year. Their modest size, generous early blossom and good manners in taking their foliage off early makes them ideal for all gardens where fussing is at a minimum.

type	Hardy bulb
size	Height at flowering 20-25cm (8-10in). They grow taller in hedgerows and other places where they need to push upwards to the light
foliage	Grey-green, appears early, dies down early
flowers	Cream pointed petals, creamy-yellow trumpets. Individuals vary a little in colour and form. Early spring
planting	Plant in early autumn in their permanent site in grass, by hedgerows, beneath trees or between shrubs. They can be left there almost forever
propagation	The bulbs will steadily increase by division, but the flowers will set plenty of seed; this is the way they increase in the wild – and in the garden if allowed
related kind	*N. obvallaris*, Tenby daffodil, golden with flatter petals and wider trumpet. 30cm (10in)

NARCISSUS CYCLAMINEUS 'JENNY'

Another *Narcissus cyclamineus* hybrid, this one opens a little later than 'Bartley' but is equally long lasting in bloom. The flowers are refined and dainty but on a robust, sturdy plant.

type	Hardy bulb
size	Height at flowering 25cm (10in)
foliage	Neat and unobtrusive
flowers	With long, pointed, swept-back white petals and a narrow trumpet pointing downwards, the flowers look graceful and sit on the back of the spring breeze. The trumpets open creamy-primrose and fade to white with age. Mid-spring
planting	Like all daffodils, it is best to plant in early autumn in informal groups, initially of perhaps six to ten bulbs
site	Excellent in grass, front of the border, between shrubs, in the heather garden or in the larger rock garden
propagation	Bulbs will increase quickly, especially in good border soil. In grass they will be somewhat slower to multiply
other cultivars	See margin

NARCISSUS 'DAYDREAM'

There are very many thousands of daffodil cultivars; 'Daydream' is a rather late-flowering one. The bright lemon colouring shines out in the garden – it also makes a lovely cut flower. It is one of the unusual ones which open with the trumpet a darker tone but end up with it nearly snow white, though the petals remain shining lemon.

type	Hardy bulb, strong
size	Height at flowering 45cm (18in)
foliage	Dark green
flowers	Rounded petals, flat and at right angles to the large cup which is almost a full trumpet length (ie as long as the petals). Mid- to late spring
planting	Plant with 10-15cm (4-6in) of soil over the bulbs
site	Excellent border plant
soil	Increases rapidly in good soil
care	Lift and replant in early summer, every three years
propagation	See panel
other cultivars	See margin

NARCISSUS 'DAYDREAM'

RECOMMENDED DAFFODIL CULTIVARS

'Falstaff', large cup, gold and scarlet, beginning of season
'Ice Wings', multi-headed **Narcissus triandrus** hybrid, several snow white, drooping heads. Mid-season
'Passionale', large cup, white and rosy pink. Late season
'St Keverne', large cup, gold. Mid daffodil season
'St Patrick's Day', large cup, wide crown, lemon. Mid-season
'Tuesday's Child', **N.** *triandrus* hybrid, two or three heads, white and yellow. Late season

NARCISSUS CYCLAMINEUS AND ITS HYBRIDS

This species grows to 15cm (6in) with yellow flowers in early to mid-spring. Damp, sandy, acid soil suits it best.
N. cyclamineus hybrids are very healthy bulbs in all soils. Choose from:

'February Gold', yellow, 25cm (10in)
'Foundling', white and pink, late, 25cm (10in)
'Ibis', white and primrose, 23cm (9in)
'Jack Snipe', white and gold, 20cm (8in)
'Jetfire', yellow and orange, 25cm (10in)
'Jumblie', golden-orange, very early, 15cm (6in)
'Tête à Tête', golden, very early, 12cm (5in)

practical project

DESIGNING AND BUILDING PATHWAYS

GARDEN ACCESS

There is little point in a splendid garden if you cannot get around it easily and safely to enjoy all its parts. Pathways are needed that are safe for walking and for conveying tools and materials, perhaps in a wheelbarrow. The garden tends to be viewed more from certain angles, such as the living room windows, than others, and it can look very different from each vantage point in the garden. The whole thing will be more exciting and varied if you can move easily through the garden to points that give you a new aspect to enjoy.

DESIGNING PATHWAYS

Paths are not just practical; they can be a major part of the garden design and attractive in themselves. Even without travelling along them we follow their lines by eye and begin to explore the space around them. The lines and proportions will therefore be very important. There will be places, maybe near the house, where straight lines will seem in keeping, but through the garden gentle curves may be more interesting and even intriguing.

Width and perspective

Normally the paths or parts of paths nearer the house will be wider than those further away, as close to the house they are going to be used more heavily and by more people. The smaller width of more distant paths can help to exaggerate this sense of distance in a small garden, making it appear bigger. This perspective effect – a visual deception – can be achieved quite adequately by narrowing, say, a 2.5m (8ft) path by only 60cm (2ft) to 2m (6ft), even over a considerable distance. If this is combined with some construction such as a pergola that becomes narrower at its far end, the effect will be considerably enhanced.

Very narrow paths can look mean and unattractive, yet almost as bad are over-wide ones out of proportion with the size of the garden.

MATERIALS

There can be arguments both for using a single material for a path and for including two or even three dissimilar materials.

Four main factors will govern the choice of materials: beauty, utility, safety and cost.

A well-made path of good York stone takes a lot of beating – and if the genuine materials are used it also takes a lot of paying for. However, there are very good imitation York stone slabs available which look almost as good, especially when they have weathered.

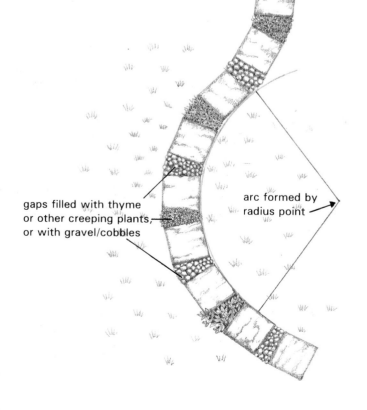

gaps filled with thyme or other creeping plants, or with gravel/cobbles

arc formed by radius point

York stone

Brick paths can look warm, be hard-wearing and link house and garden. Choose kinds such as blue engineering bricks that will stand wear and weathering. Decide on herring-bone or other patterns.

LAYING THE PATH

■ Mark out pathway with string or canes. Leave for a few days to see whether modifications seem advisable.

■ Decide on materials. A hard working path could be of paving stones, brick, or gravel. Gravel or stones may be bordered by bricks, imitation brick blocks or 'Victorian' black-blue rope edging.

■ Remove turf or top few cms/ins of soil. Level the area so that completed path will be flush with its surrounds. Ensure that it will not be liable to persistent damp or lying rain water at any point.

■ Add a layer 4–5cm (1½–2in) deep of washed sand which is excellent for the base of most domestic paths. Rake it to provide an even base for the path material.

■ Paths to bear much traffic may need a hardcore base of 15cm (6in) of rammed gravel beneath paving slabs bedded on 4–5cm (1½–2in) of mortar. Use a generous trowel's worth of mortar at each corner and in the centre of each large slab. Only with exceptionally heavy traffic is a complete layer of mortar necessary.

■ Lay bricks or slabs flat or with a slight fall so the path will shed water to the side where it can drain away.

■ Where there is less traffic and possibly away from the immediate vicinity of the house, a hardwearing dry route can be made by dropping slabs or stones into a lawn. Try walking along the route so that you feel happy with the distance between the slabs. Ensure that they end level with the grass and will not be hit by the grass cutter.

soldier courses

herringbone

stretcher bond

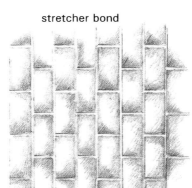

basketweave

herringbone

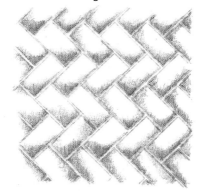

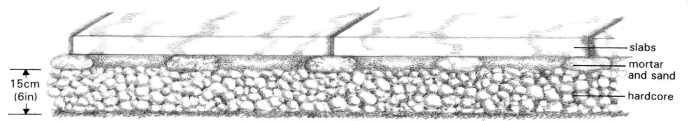

15cm
(6in)

slabs
mortar and sand
hardcore

hardwearing path for heavier traffic

plants
OF THE
month

RECOMMENDED
TULIP SPECIES

Tulipa fosteriana, huge, scarlet
T. humilis, dwarf, violet-pink,
yellow base
T. kolpakowskiana (see profile)
T. linifolia, dwarf, blazing deep red
T. sprengeri, latest, tall, orange
T. tarda, see profile
T. turkestanica, late winter, small,
white and yellow
T. urumiensis, dwarf, like **T. tarda**
but all gold

RECOMMENDED
TULIP CULTIVARS

KAUFMANNIANAS
'Ancilla', soft pink and white
'Giuseppe Verdi', cherry, edged
yellow
'Heart's Delight', rose, red and
yellow
'Shakespeare', small, salmon
shades
'Stresa', slender yellow and red

TULIPS

In the first few years of this century it was the fashion for huge numbers of tulips to be planted each autumn and then lifted and maybe even discarded after flowering. Bedding out was done in large numbers, but economics, smaller gardens and altered tastes have wrought big changes. Tulips are still used for some bedding but usually they are employed tactically in groups in the border, between shrubs or in containers.

Early-flowering dwarf Tulipa kaufmanniana *hybrids and slightly later ones with more* T. greigii *blood in them stand sturdy, some 10-25cm (4-10in) high with pointed flower buds and a range of brilliant colours. They are great value in early spring. In very well-drained soils in sunny sites, bulbs planted 15cm (6in) or even deeper can usually be left for several years without lifting.*

The huge hybrids between the old Darwins and T. fosteriana *are very robust and are marketed as 'Darwin Hybrids'. Patches have been known to make their territory colourful for over ten seasons completely untended.*

Some tulip species do well without lifting and fussing provided they have excellent drainage and grow in full light conditions. Particularly good are T. tarda, T. praestans, T. humilis *and* T. sprengeri.

TULIPA 'WHITE TRIUMPHATOR'

This is a most impressive, tallish tulip of the lily-flowered class, wonderful in the garden border between herbaceous plants or shrubs. A group can have something of the same magic as a frozen tableau in a ballet.

type	Bulb with tunic. Lily-flowered tulip
size	Height at flowering 60cm (2ft)
foliage	Grey-green, wide leaves – almost hostas!
flowers	Firm-petalled, pure white with pointed petals curving outwards. Mid- to late spring
planting	Plant in autumn with at least 12cm (5in) soil over the bulbs
site	Open, airy spot in full light
soil	Warm, well drained
care	Keep clear of weeds
propagation	Lift in early summer, clean the bulbs, and keep dry and cool. Replant mid- to late autumn.

TULIPA 'WHITE TRIUMPHATOR'

	Alternatively, lift, split up the bulbs, clean and replant immediately
other cultivars	See margin (Lily-flowered)

TULIPA PRAESTANS 'FUSILIER'

type	Hardy bulb
size	Height at flowering 20-25cm (8-10in)
foliage	Light green
flowers	Three to five blooms to a stem, cleanly cut cup-shaped flowers uniformly coloured a bright, rich orange. Mid-spring
planting	Plant in autumn in an airy spot with good drainage, if possible where the bulbs can be 'baked' in summer
site	Towards the front of the border, possibly between shrubs, in the rock garden, in containers or even in gravelled areas
propagation	The strong bulbs increase well when they feel at home
other cultivars	'Tubergen's variety', a little dwarfer, two or three orange flowers per stem. 'Zwanenburg variety', 30cm (12in), several deep crimson flowers

TULIPA 'JEWEL OF SPRING'

One of many fine large Darwin Hybrids that are exceptionally strong garden plants.

type	Hardy bulb. Darwin Hybrid
size	Height at flowering 60cm (2ft)
foliage	Huge, wide lower leaves like hostas, rather smaller stem leaves. Light green
flowers	Massive sulphur/lemon-yellow blooms with a greenish-black basal blotch. Very fine pencilled margin of red to each petal. A sport from the yellow-and-orange 'Gudoshnik'
planting	Plant in autumn deeply and at least 20cm (8in) apart
site	Best in an open, sunny spot
soil	Well cultivated
care	Remove dead heads and foliage as it fails. A very strong plant. If left in the ground for several years the flowers are smaller than their huge first-year size but still remarkable
propagation	Bulbs increase steadily in number and may need lifting every few years to give them more room
other cultivars	See margin (Darwin Hybrids)

TULIPA PRAESTANS 'FUSILIER'

TULIPA KOLPAKOWSKIANA

TULIPA KOLPAKOWSKIANA

type	Small bulb, tough tunic
size	Height at flowering 15cm (6in)
foliage	Narrow, low-lying leaves, the strongest only about 2.5cm (1in) wide but possibly up to 20cm (8in) long
flowers	Relatively large with pointed petals, the outer three flushed pink outside, otherwise the whole flower a bright mid-yellow without any central blotch. At first a cup or vase shape but opening to a star
site	Well-drained rock garden where it will prove hardy and easy to grow. Alternatively, grow in a container or towards the front of a border

TULIPA TARDA

type	Hardy bulb
size	Height at flowering 5-10cm (2-4in)
foliage	Bright polished green leaves in a rosette on the ground
flowers	Virtually stemless green buds open to white and gold stars nestling in the centre. Mid- to late spring
planting	Plant in autumn 10-15cm (4-6in) deep
site	Open, sunny spot in the border or rock garden
soil	Well drained
propagation	Bulbs will increase steadily over the years and can be lifted and divided every two or three seasons

RECOMMENDED TULIP CULTIVARS

GREIGIIS
'Cape Cod', yellow, orange and red
'Corsage', orange, pink and yellow
'Oriental Beauty', brilliant vermilion
'Plaisir', creamy-yellow striped rosy-red
'Red Riding Hood', scarlet with purple-striped leaves

LILY-FLOWERED
'China Pink', pink with white base
'Mariette', rose with well-reflexed petal tips
'West Point', slender, primrose yellow
'White Triumphator', see profile

DARWIN HYBRIDS
'Apeldoorn', scarlet red
'Apeldoorn's Elite', orange-red on yellow
'Jewel of Spring', see profile
'Golden Apeldoorn', deep gold
'Spring Song', crimson

practical project

GROUND-COVER PLANTING

PLANTS FOR GROUND COVER

FOR DRY SOIL
Alchemilla mollis, lady's mantle
Ballota pseudodictamnus
Brunnera macrophylla
Euphorbia robbiae
Hedera, ivies

FOR WET/MOIST SOIL
Blechnum spicant, hard fern
Most other ferns
Geranium 'Johnson's Blue'
G. macrorrhizum
Hosta, all

FOR SHADE
Epimedium perralderianum
Euphorbia robbiae
Geranium phaeum
Hedera, ivies
Pachysandra terminalis
Tiarella cordifolia foam flower

GROUND-COVER RULES

Ground-cover plants should be:
- *Absolutely hardy;*
- *rapid and tenacious growers, but not rumbustious extrovert characters wishing to dominate all;*
- *tolerant of the garden conditions;*
- *virtually maintenance free;*
- *plants that you enjoy and which have more than just a passing claim to beauty.*

To carry out a ground-covering scheme does not mean that *all* the plants must fulfil these five criteria. The ground can be covered, but it will also allow us to plant bulbs, trees, and other shrubs and herbaceous plants as 'stars'. If this sounds as if the ground-coverers are mere background players, this may be the impression on paper, but in the garden every plant plays its part and is admired.

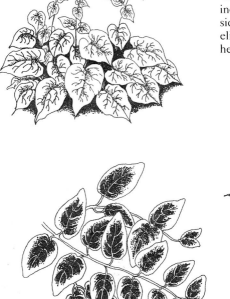

PLANNING AN AREA OF GROUND COVER

The aim is to plant a bed, border or other patch of ground with a selection of plants that will manage themselves and keep all weeds at bay.

- Eliminate all perennial weeds before carrying out any planting.

- Cultivate the soil thoroughly. The plants may be tough but they need the same good start as newly introduced specimens.

- Except for occasional solo turns, install your chosen plants in groups of a kind, so that they can stake their claim to an area.

- To get quick cover, plant your specimens rather closer than normal.

- Keep the bed weed free in the weeks and months that the plants take to establish themselves.

- Sit back and enjoy the ensemble.

CHOICE OF PLANTS

The choice of plants is of course yours; the lists include first-rate kinds that ought to be considered. Normal shrub-shaped shrubs are eligible but for reasons of space are not listed here.

THE GROUND-COVER ARGUMENT

The idea is simple, and the sort of logic to appeal to the easy gardener: if the ground is covered with plants the weeds will not get a look in. Proponents point to the fact that nature never leaves a bare piece of soil. The argument is almost too simple and complete. Then the clincher is thrown in: it's cheap.

The fact is that a garden is an artificial thing; you are holding the line against the threatening horde of nature's in-fillers. Of course, if you can work *with* nature so much to the good; to avoid extra work and perhaps frustration you should grow those plants that do well in your soils and conditions. This is something the ground-covering gurus will agree with, but the more ardent will then start listing the plants that can be used for ground cover and you begin to feel that the enthusiasm is too great – almost every ornamental plant is given points as a ground coverer. To be so inclusive means that the argument collapses on itself.

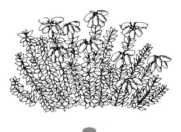

GROUND-COVERING PLANTS

You can cover the ground by planting many plants close together or by using those with a recognised potential to colonise and cover.

The dense canopy of beech trees in a wood prevents much undergrowth. In the garden this has to be scaled down, using shrubs to provide thick cover, either evergreen or deciduous (the leaf-droppers will create their weed-inhibiting canopy in the months when weed germination and growth is most active).

A balance between shrubs and strong herbaceous plants should create the necessary cover. The herbaceous ground-coverers fall roughly into two categories: the obvious energetic colonisers such as *Euphorbia robbiae*, and strong clump-formers such as hostas. Shrubby plants also tend to fall into two groups: those that carpet the ground, like heathers or *Euonymus fortunei* cultivars, and taller plants with spreading branches, such as rhododendrons, pieris or laurel, which create fairly impenetrable shade below.

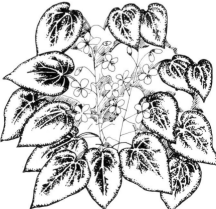

PLANTS FOR GROUND COVER

EVERGREEN HERBACEOUS
Bergenia cordifolia and the stronger *Bergenia* cultivars
Helleborus agutifolius
H. orientalis cultivars
H. foetidus
Tellima grandiflora rubra

SHRUBBY CARPETING PLANTS
Artemisia stelleriana
Calluna vulgaris (heather)
Cistus parviflora
Cotoneaster dammeri
C. 'Gnom' and other low-growing cultivars
Cytisus × kewensis, broom
C. scoparius maritimus
Erica carnea, winter-flowering heather
Euonymus fortunei cultivars
Vinca major periwinkle
V. minor

SPOT PLANTS
Ferns
Ornamental grasses
Acanthus mollis
Genista hispanica, Spanish broom
G. lydia

ROCK PLANTS/SMALL CARPETERS
Acaena novae-zelandiae
Ajuga reptans, bugle
Aubrieta
Hebe pinguifolia 'Pagei' and other low hebes
Persicarpa affinis cultivars
Phlox subulata
P. douglasii
Polygonum affine (syn. Persicarpa affinis)
Mossy saxifrages
Thymus serpyllum

MAY

*Late spring and nearly summer. The garden is in full season,
hedgerows and the shrubs and trees in our gardens are fully
clothed, garden visiting and flower-show time is here again.
Which won, the first cuckoo or the first hosepipe ban? In winter the
need for water may not have seemed pressing, but it would have
been prudent to have installed as many waterbutts to collect
rainfall from house, shed and greenhouse roofs as practicable.
Certainly gardeners should at least have given some thought to
saving water and to ensuring that their plants will be looked
after. In drier gardens this may mean foregoing the pleasures of
some plants that are heavy drinkers. Look instead towards those
that can manage drought better, perhaps the stronger
Mediterranean plants, but you need not miss out on glamour and
colour when plants like lilies are remarkably resistant to periods
of drought. Late spring can often coincide with a surprisingly long
period without significant rain, and gardeners ought to be
prepared.*

*The sound of lawn mowers is loud in the land, hedges are being
clipped, the vegetable grower is losing sweat. But the owner of the
easy garden is sitting without any quibbles of conscience, work
ethic fully under control; the view is being admired, the birds
listened to, the radio is on . . .*

*Whilst shrubs and alpines are in expansive decorative form and
many bulbs are still strongly in colourful evidence, the more
precocious ones are fading fast. In the borders the herbaceous
heavyweights are making ready, paeonies, lupins and delphiniums
jostling with thrusting stems of lilies. We live in exciting times.*

tasks
FOR THE
month

ARGYRANTHEMUMS
Hanging baskets as well as ground-borne containers will be enlivened by argyranthemums. 'Jamaica Primrose' is a popular kind that is hugely generous with its soft yellow daisies through the sunnier months. They can be very effective in the border as well as in large jardinières and pots.

CHECKLIST

☐ Remove spring bedding
☐ Review your containers, planting up and replanting as necessary
☐ Prune spring-flowering shrubs
☐ Continue with your weed-control programme
☐ Spray roses against mildew, blackspot and rust
☐ Continue to wage war against aphids and slugs
☐ Apply and top up mulches as necessary

SPRING BEDDING

Easy gardening does not cater for a lot of bedding, but room can be found for a few wallflowers, forget-me-nots and even such frippery as overblown daisies, *Bellis perennis* cultivars – it would certainly be a depleted spring without the scent and velvety colours of wallflowers. But now these temporary plants will have had their day and they can be pulled up and composted.

REVIEWING CONTAINERS

Containers that held spring bulbs and winter pansies will need emptying and renewing. Any that have been out of commission over winter can now be brought back into use. Those holding permanent plants, say conifers or shrubs, should at least have their topsoil scraped off and replaced with fresh compost.

Half-hardy perennials like geraniums (pelargoniums) can now be hardened off. There is no disputing the value of these plants; in containers they will thrive and bloom for months with little attention apart from making sure that they do not dry out completely, more than repaying the small effort of keeping them frost-free over winter. If you shun the brilliant carnival colours, the reds and shouting oranges, there are plenty of cooler colours, in the white to pale pink range. There are also the scented-leaved kinds that are very decorative even if you do not press their leaves to release the perfume.

Taking plants from a heated greenhouse or warm kitchen windowsill straight out to an exposed spot on the patio can court trouble; frost and biting winds are not unknown in late spring. The plants ought to be brought first into a cool spot to harden off, a halfway house, before being turned out into a container or a raised bed to do their summer duty. A cold frame, porch, car-port or space beneath a sheltered wall can be the spot to harden off these and other half-hardy plants.

If purchasing from garden centres try to ensure that you have plants that have been properly hardened off. Saving your own plants from year to year is possible, but it does require space, time and some insulation of the plants from winter frosting. You may decide it is easier and cheaper to purchase fresh each season. At this time of year the garden centres have been full of bedding and container plants for weeks – often long before even moderately prudent gardeners would consider introducing them to outdoor life. If you buy early, grow the plants on in cool conditions and then harden them off for planting out towards the end of the month.

Feeding and watering

Hanging baskets mean a fair measure of work throughout the summer, unless you can adopt easy watering and feeding methods. Feeding is the lesser problem, especially if you incorporate slow-release fertilisers with the compost when planting up the containers. You can also introduce gel products (readily available from garden centres) that help conserve water.

The basic truth, however, is that containers must not be allowed to dry out, and the larger the container the easier it is to maintain a

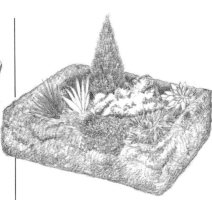

NOTE

■ *There may be a choice of small plants grown in 'plugs' of compost in moulded plastic module trays; these mini-plants are likely to be healthy when first offered and are cheaper than full-size plants. However, sometimes they are not cared for as well as they might be and can become a little tired. Unless you enjoy growing these little plants to full size it may be a false economy, and you may be better advised to purchase more mature plants* ■

reasonable amount of moisture and an equable soil temperature. These are prerequisites for a balanced collection of plants that is going to look well for months rather than a week or two.

Movable containers

Buy or make the largest containers you can afford and that look appropriate to their setting. If you can, have one or two in the wings waiting to take centre stage when their plants are ready and the containers currently on show are beginning to look tired. This means that the containers must be movable. Always raise the really large containers slightly above the ground to allow for easy drainage, prevent access for pests, and, more importantly, to enable a sack-truck, rollers or planks to be positioned underneath to aid movement.

PRUNING SPRING-FLOWERING SHRUBS

Forsythias may already have

been pruned; if not, they should join the other strong spring-flowering shrubs in having heavily flowered and older wood cut back to low buds to encourage fresh growth on which next year's blossom will be borne.

CONTROLLING WEEDS

Strong growth in the lawn makes this an ideal time to spray weeds with selective hormone weedkiller, ie one that does not affect grass but systematically kills broad-leaved plants.

Continue to run the hoe through small germinating weeds in the borders to save a lot of work later. Any bad perennial weeds that are threatening to establish themselves can be killed with a glyphosate systemic weedkiller using a hand-held sprayer with the nozzle

arranged to hit only the offending weed.

SPRAYING ROSES AND CONTROLLING PESTS

A fungicide sprayed over the foliage of roses will pre-empt attacks of mildew, blackspot and rust. With a further spray in a month's time you will have gone a long way to keeping your plants clear for another year.

Small outbreaks of aphids may be dealt with by birds, ladybirds and other predators. Check the growing points and buds of roses, a favourite first attack site. If aphid numbers build up, they can be dealt with using an insecticide spray. If you hate using manufactured insecticides, a few assaults with water generously laced with detergent will often deal satisfactorily with the pests. (See p33 for slug control.)

MULCHING

Top up shredded bark layers where they are thinning near to vanishing point. Top dress with gravel in the rock garden and troughs. If you have plenty of well-rotted compost this can be used very beneficially as a mulch 5-8cm (2-3in) deep around delphiniums, paeonies, lilies and other strong growers before the end of the month.

CUTTING THE GRASS
Do not set the cutting blades of your mower too low: it is better to have 5cm (2in) of growth on the lawn than to risk brown patches from drought at this time of year.

SNOWDROPS AND WINTER ACONITES
Finish lifting, splitting and replanting these useful early-flowering bulbs by the end of the month to build up numbers for future years.

M A Y

plants
OF THE
month

BEGINNER'S ROCK-GARDEN COLLECTION

The following are all easy, reliable and very attractive plants:

Achillea clavennae
Alyssum saxatile
Androsace sarmentosa
Antennaria rosea
Campanula portenschlagiana
Dianthus 'Bourboule'
Iberis sempervirens 'Weisser Zwerg'
Iris pumila
Phlox subulata
Primula marginata
Saponaria ocymoides
Saxifraga paniculata forms
Sempervivium arachnoideum
S. tectorum forms
Thymus serpyllum forms

ROCK-GARDEN PLANTS

Whilst there are plenty of rock-garden plants – alpines – that bloom and look good at other times of the year, the spring is the period of greatest floral interest. Most are mountain dwellers that may have been covered with snow for months and have to run through their annual cycle of flowering, growing and seeding before the early return of winter conditions. They are plants in a hurry, and as soon as the snow and ice retreats they rush into bright bloom. These plants are primarily suited to the rock garden or bed, but can also be used in the border. Certainly this applies to the stronger primulas, such as P. denticulata.

DRUMSTICK PRIMULA
(Primula denticulata)

type	Hardy herbaceous perennial
size	Height at flowering 15-35cm (6-14in); seeding stems elongate
foliage	Mid-green, long, oval and serrated. In a choice spot leaves can look rather gross in summer
flower	Large, round 'drumstick' heads of bloom, from pure white through lavender tones to a rich burgundy red. Late spring
site	Open site. Tolerates light shade
soil	Not fussy provided soil does not dry out
care	Very easy plant
propagation	Simply raised from seed. Good colour forms can be propagated from 2.5cm (1in) lengths of thick root placed in pots of all-purpose compost in early spring

PRIMULA DENTICULATA

GERANIUM CINEREUM 'BALLERINA'

Hardy geraniums, not the bedding pelargoniums, are amongst the most trouble-free of plants. This is true of both the larger herbaceous kinds and the smaller plants for the rock garden, like the variety described here.

type	Hardy herbaceous perennial with a thick rootstock
size	Height 10cm (4in), spread 30cm (12in)
foliage	Basal leaves of semi-evergreen rosettes, rounded but deeply cut, soft textured, grey-green. Dies down to a fat winter bud
flowers	Wide, bowl-shaped blooms of mauvy-pink, with a network of deep purple veins more intricate at the margins and more heavily drawn towards the purple-black centres. Late spring and well into summer
site	Excellent in a rock garden or bed, or could be placed at the front of a border
soil	Reasonably well drained
care	Easy in suitable soils. Plant in early spring
other cultivars	'Lawrence Flatman', compact free flowering; 'Album', white

SAXIFRAGA 'PIXIE'

The saxifrage genus is a huge one, crowded with interesting and beautiful rock-garden plants. By far the easiest to start with are the 'mossy' kinds, like 'Pixie', the quick-growing plants soon making attractive green mats and blooming freely in spring. One of a series of care-free cultivars with flowers in colours from white to dark red and with stems varying in height from 1-15cm (⅓-6in).

type	Evergreen carpeting perennial
size	Height 7-10cm (3-4in), spread 45cm (18in)
foliage	Evergreen, bright green, ending each of the many stems with a rosette of leaves deeply divided into pointed lobes
flowers	The mat of foliage is lost behind a mass of upturned bells of rosey-red on short stems in mid- and late spring
site	In full light
soil	Reasonably well drained
care	Very easy-going plants. Plant

propagation spring. Can be trimmed back if they spread too far

propagation Whilst seed will provide a range of forms, cultivars can be propagated easily from cuttings 2.5cm (1in) long in late spring. (Good cuttings are induced by covering a small portion with an upturned pot; stems elongate to give more handy cuttings. Remove the lower leaves)

PASQUE FLOWER
(Pulsatilla vulgaris)
(formerly *Anemone pulsatilla*)

The pulsatillas have been given generic status after many years listed as anemones. They are all delightful plants, but of all the species *Pulsatilla vulgaris* is the easiest and showiest in the open garden.

type Hardy perennial dying down in winter to a tufted, woody rootstock

size Height and spread 15-23cm (6-9in)

foliage Attractive deeply divided, ferny, light green foliage, silver with hairs in youth

flowers Large, nodding blooms through spring. Usually mid-purple but there are also white, silvery-grey, lavender, pinky-mauve and red forms, all with a central boss of golden stamens. Stems grow longer and have decorative feathery seedheads

site Best in full sun

soil We l drained

care Long-lived, easy plant

propagation Fresh seed germinates readily. Good colour forms are propagated by root cuttings taken in late summer or winter; insert 2.5cm (1in) lengths of fleshy roots at least 3mm (⅛in) thick right end up in gritty potting compost. Over winter in a cold frame or protected cool spot. The plants will be ready for potting on in spring

cultivars *P.v.* alba, white; *P.v.* rubra, ruby red

BELLFLOWER
(Campanula carpatica)

Campanulas range from tiny, tiny plants from mountain tops to large herbaceous plants reaching up to 2m (6ft). There are many good,

PULSATILLA VULGARIS RUBRA

easy rock-garden species, but some spread invasively by underground stems; these happy wanderers can be very attractive in walls and paving. *Campanula carpatica* is easy, showy but manageable.

type Hardy, clump-forming perennial with many branching stems and leaves dying back to a central rootstock for winter

size Height 8-10cm (3-4in), spread 30cm (12in)

foliage Light green, oval to rounded leaves with some serration

flowers Large, wide, upward-facing bells in rich blue; there are also deeper violet-blue and paler forms, as well as pure whites in late spring

site Open rock garden or bed, or an airy spot in sun or shade (not too dense)

soil Moist but well drained. A gritty compost works well

care Easy

propagation From seed or softwood/basal cuttings in summer. Seed will give some variation in colour shades

cultivars 'Blue Clips', compact with many wide mid-blue bells; 'White Clips', shining white counterpart

DWARF CONIFERS AND SHRUBS

A few of these make all the difference to a collection of alpines; they are particularly useful in winter.

CONIFERS
Chamaecyparis obtusa 'Nana Gracilis'
C.o. 'Tetragona aurea'
Cryptomeria japonica 'Vilmoriniana'
Juniperus communis 'Compressa'
Thuya orientalis 'Aurea nana'

SHRUBBY PLANTS
Genista lydia
Hebe pinguifolia 'Pagei'
Hypericum olympicum minus
Salix lanata
S. reticulata
Veronica fruticans

M A Y

practical project

MAKING ROCKERY BEDS

LIME-TOLERANT ROCK-GARDEN PLANTS

Acantholimon • Acanthus
Achillea ageratifolia
A. clavennae • Aethionema
Aubrieta • Cyclamen
Dianthus • Dryas octopetala
Gentiana clusii • G. saxosa
Globularia • Gypsophila
Helleborus • Potentilla nitida
Primula auricula
P. marginata
Pulsatilla (not *P. vernalis*)
Saxifraga

LIME-HATING ROCK-GARDEN PLANTS

Achillea moschata
A. nana
Astrantia minor
Campanula excisa
Chrysanthemum alpinum
Dianthus glacialis
D. microlepis
Dicentra cucullaria
D. eximia
Douglasia
Gentiana (most)
Haplopappus brandegeei
Helichrysum frigidum
Houstonia

Trying to create a natural-looking rock garden in a space dominated by buildings and other artificial garden features can be difficult; a rockery bed can fit into the general design much more easily and be far simpler to work and maintain. Rockery beds have many advantages:

▪ The plants are not so far down and can be reached from the sides. Accessibility can be a boon to less active gardeners.

▪ The beds can provide ideal conditions for a wide range of alpines.

▪ Paving or other good, safe standing ground can surround the structure.

▪ The growing media can be regulated more easily. Drainage is easily provided.

▪ The walls themselves will provide a variety of different planting sites.

▪ Without the need to invest in large pieces of rock, the cost will be much less than for a rock garden.

▪ Maintenance will be easier than with a rock garden.

▪ Smaller plants can be seen and appreciated very much better.

DESIGN AND MATERIALS

A bed may lack the sculptural feel of a rock garden but can still be very attractive. The walls should be pleasing to the eye, and plants growing in them and spilling over from the tops will banish any feeling of harshness. The walls can act almost like a frame around a picture.

Various materials can be used to build the walls of a rockery bed. Layers of rock will look good, but bricks, tree branches, logs or peat-blocks will all work well. Your choice will depend on what is available and what will look right in your garden. Do not dismiss the idea of railway sleepers, either: you will have the wall built in a trice, and with plants clambering over them they can look really good.

Whilst a rectangle is the obvious shape, with the width no greater than the distance you can reach comfortably from the sides (perhaps 2m (6ft)), an L-shaped form may also fit in well. Normally the bed will be of a uniform height all over, but it could be built against a bankside or an existing wall, when the top could slope. A level-topped bed can be modified to include two or more levels as a terraced effect, with extra walls constructed from bricks or rocks. A rockery bed cannot be anything but an artificial construction, but it looks better and the plants more at home with some rocks placed in the top.

TIMESCALE

▪ *Take your time over this project. The finished bed will last a long time, so it is better to have it correctly and securely constructed than to hurry the building process. Think in terms of two or three weekends* ▪

SITING

The bed should be positioned in the light and away from dripping trees. It can stand on the soil or on hardstanding. On concrete or other more-or-less impervious materials, some thought must be given to drainage, not just for

soil level

the plants within the bed but of the whole. Otherwise, there could be constant seepage of water on to the hardstanding around the bed, especially after periods of very wet weather.

CONSTRUCTION

■ Site drainage should be good. On concrete or compact clay it may be necessary to lead water to a lower level with field drains.

■ Bury the first course of building materials 2.5-5cm (1-2in) below ground level to anchor the wall.

■ Lay the second course so that the joins of the first level pieces are bridged. If rocks are used, the wall will look best if the rocks in a particular course are all of approximately the same depth. Courses can be of differing depths.

■ Ensure that the finished height suits both the gardener and the site. On well-drained soils a rockery bed need consist of only a single course of brick or stone, but a convenient height is 30-60cm (1-2ft).

■ A slight battering (sloping) of the sides is helpful but not essential; walls leaning inwards

will be a little more secure. If the top surfaces or stones lean back a little there will be some intake of rainfall.

■ An occasional large rock or stone should project into the bed to help maintain the rigidity of the structure.

■ As the walls are built up, begin to fill the bed; first with a layer of drainage material, then with a gritty soil/compost mix, and finally with a layer of chippings to finish off.

LIME-HATING ROCK-GARDEN PLANTS

Lewisia
Lithodora diffusa
Lychnis alpina
Penstemon (most)
Potentilla aurea
Pulsatilla vernalis
Saponaria pumilio
Saxifraga cotyledon
S. cortusifolia
S. lilacina
Sempervivium montanum
S. wulfenii

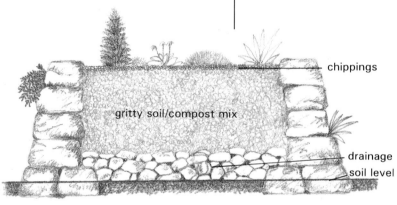

chippings

gritty soil/compost mix

drainage

soil level

M A Y

plants
OF THE
month

FERNS

These wonderful plants dominated the earth before flowering plants evolved. There are still huge numbers in most parts of the world and many are hardy in temperate areas. There are evergreen and deciduous sorts, plus some that are deciduous in hard winters but can otherwise be evergreen. They can range in size from little wall species like the maidenhair spleenwort (Asplenium trichomanes) to the huge Royal fern (Osmunda regalis).

Ferns can be propagated from spores collected from the backs of fertile fronds or by division. However, young nursery plants are so reasonably priced that this is often the most practical way of acquiring one or two more.

ADIANTUM PEDATUM

ROYAL FERN
(Osmunda regalis)

type	Hardy, deciduous, long-lived perennial dying down to a steadily enlarging, tufted, creeping rootstock. Rare British native
size	By midsummer an established clump can be several metres across and much taller than a man
fronds	Individual fronds can be well over 2m (6ft) long and 1m (3ft) across in damp sites. They have been measured to as much as 4m (12ft) long in very favoured, damp, sheltered sites. Even in very much less lush spots this is still an impressive plant with fronds 60cm-1m (2-3ft) long. Particularly attractive in mid- and late spring, when stems reach up and the 'croziers' begin to unfurl
planting	Small pot grown plants can be placed in their quarters at any time but will probably do best if planted in spring
site	Ideally by a pond or stream, otherwise as damp as possible. Needs room to develop and make its theatrical statement
soil	damp
care	Given moisture, this is an impressive, care-free plant. Frost rusts the green fronds, but the tumbling mass of fawny brown is not without beauty through most of the winter. The tidy minded will clear any old fronds at the end of winter before the new ones arise

AMERICAN MAIDENHAIR FERN
(Adiantum pedatum)

type	Deciduous, hardy, creeping rhizomatous perennial. A distinctive species of which all forms are pleasing
size	Variable. Height normally 30-50cm (12-20in)
fronds	Very slender, almost black, wiry erect stems carry fronds nearly horizontally. Each frond is almost parallel sided, with a series of oblong blades fitted as if to a fan. A rich but matt green
site	Best in cool, moist shade
soil	Acid, but tolerant of a range of soils
care	Once established, spreads steadily
propagation	Clumps can be divided easily in spring
cultivars	*A.p. subpumilum*, a half-sized form

SCALY MALE FERN

(Dryopteris affinis 'Grandiceps Askew')

The scaly male fern is widely distributed through SW Asia and Europe, including Britain. The type is a strong tufted plant with rather erect, narrow fronds reaching from near the ground to some 50cm-1.5m (20in-5ft) in length.

type	Hardy, semi-evergreen, long-lived tufted perennial
size	Height and spread 60-90cm (2-3ft)
fronds	Very elongated, triangular, much-divided fronds ending in crests, but also crested at the ends of the pinnae (divisions) down the frond margins. Yellowish green when young but soon a rich shade
planting	Plant spring.
site	Best in shade or semi-shade
soil	Thrives in damp, humus-rich soils but is tolerant of drier, poorer spots
care	Grows robustly in most situations and soils
propagation	Two- or three-year-old plants can be divided into a few pieces in spring just as they are about to get into active growth again. Never try to divide ferns into very small pieces
cultivars	*D.a.* 'Cristata The King', 50-90cm (20-36in), firm textured, parallel-sided fronds very evenly divided and crested the whole length and end

HART'S TONGUE FERN

(Asplenium scolopendrium 'Marginatum'*)*

The typical native hart's tongue fern is one of the joys of the countryside of Asia, North America and Europe, including Britain, where it is particularly plentiful in the moister western side. The standard form, and mutants like 'Marginatum', are excellent garden plants, especially useful in damp, shaded areas and awkward spots where little else flourishes.

type	Hardy, evergreen, tufted perennial native
size	Height and spread 20-30cm (8-12in)
fronds	Twelve months of shining, rich glossy green fronds, narrower than the type and much cut into into and waved
site	Best in shade or semi-shade
soil	Damp
care	Grows easily in places where it is not subject to drought
propagation	After two or three years clumps can be divided in early to mid-spring
other cultivars	*A.s.* 'Crispum', with fronds goffered

ASPLENIUM SCOLOPENDRIUM 'MARGINATUM'

FERNS TO TRY
For suggestions for other ferns to try, see this month's project on making a fern border

practical project

MAKING A FERN BORDER

A CHOICE OF FERNS

Do not be daunted by the formidable names of some of these ferns – you do not have to remember them once you have bought your plants!

DWARF HARDY FERNS
(8-30cm (3-12in) tall)
Asplenium scolopendrium **'Marginata Irregulare'**, hart's tongue form
Athyrium filix-femina **'Congestum Minus'**, dwarf lady fern
Blechnum penna-marina, a colonising kind similar to the British hard fern *B. spicant*
Polypodium vulgare **'Cornubiense'**, polypody
Polystichum setiferum **'Congestum'**, dwarf soft shield fern
Polystichum tsus-simense, neat with tough, triangular fronds

WHY FERNS?

A fern border may or may not be filled only with ferns. Usually there will be some companion plants, but it is the ferns that will dominate and with the right selection, and very little work, there will be something of interest at all times of the year. There are gardens with fern borders some decades old where the only work undertaken is to remove the odd weed and sometimes clear away dead fronds.

A single fern is a thing of beauty, a collection soon begins to create an atmosphere quite distinct from any other gardening feature. These are timeless plants, they have some of the stillness of ages uncluttered by man's frenetic activity; they dominated the world over 200 million years ago, well before the first of the flowering plants. Their beauty is undeniable, but so is their usefulness.

WHERE?

There are ferns that will flourish in open, dryish conditions, but most hardy kinds are at their best in shaded or semi-shaded places that are sheltered and reasonably moist. Ferns do not need rich soils and, once planted, like to be left undisturbed as they are very much surface rooters.

With the increased density of building in towns, cities and indeed almost everywhere, more and more plots are denied much or even any sun, and often the best soil has been ruined or looted. If such an awkward site is also sheltered from wind, here you can plant ferns.

HOW?

■ Eliminate all perennial weeds.

■ Dig over the surface soil.

■ Place the ferns to be planted in their sites, remembering that some of the pretty ferns purchased in small pots may eventually become quite large. Most labels will give the ultimate size.

■ Some may be planted singly, others, such as some of the polypodys, are probably better in threes or bigger groups.

■ Plant firmly and keep moist. Do not bury the plants but set them at the same level or very slightly lower than they were in their pots.

■ Make sure the selection of ferns includes a balance of evergreen and deciduous kinds.

■ A few shrubs will add variety and provide some shelter.

■ At the appropriate time some dwarf, permanent bulbs can be added; snowdrops, cyclamen and autumn crocuses look right with the ferns.

■ If herbaceous plants are to be included, do not go wild with your selection. It is better to restrict yourself to, say, a number of good hellebores; they have 'class' and will fit in well with the ferny ambiance.

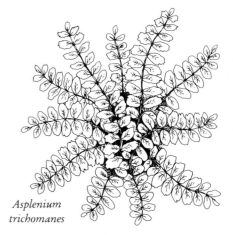

Asplenium ceterach

Asplenium trichomanes

TOP TEN FERNS

plant	frond length	description
AMERICAN MAIDENHAIR *(Adiantum pedatum.)*	30–50cm (12–20in)	Thin wiry stems. Parallel-sided fronds (see Plants of the Month)
HART'S TONGUE *(Asplenium scolopendrium)*	20–60cm (8–24in)	Evergreen, uncut shining short stemmed fronds (see Plants of the Month)
LADY FERN FORM *(Athyrium filix-femina* 'Victoriae')	25–95cm (10–38in)	Very finely divided fronds with pinnae paired as crosses and each crested
MALE FERN FORM *(Dryopteris affinis* 'Grandiceps Askew')	40–150cm (16–60in)	Majestic upright fronds crested along length and at end (see Plants of the Month)
MALE FERN FORM *(D.a.* 'Cristata The King')	40–120cm (16–48in)	Spendid upright and arching almost parallel-sided fronds elaborately crested at end of pinnae and end
AUTUMN FERN *(D. erythrosorus)*	20–50cm (8–20in)	Younger fronds are a lovely orangey-bronze. Neat triangular fronds
OSTRICH FEATHER FERN *(Matteuccia struthiopteris)*	50cm–1.5m (20in–5ft)	Also called Shuttlecock fern because upright fronds make a cylinder like a huge shuttlecock. Colonises by vigorous stolons just below soil surface
ROYAL FERN *(Osmunda regalis)*	30cm–3m (1–10ft)	Huge moisture-loving fern (see Plants of the Month)
BROAD BUCKLER FERN *(Dryopteris dilatata)*	30–150cm (12–60in)	Strong, dark triangular fronds. Loves moisture. Impressive where there is not space for royal fern
SOFT SHIELD FERN FORM *(Polystichum setiferum* 'Pulcherrimum Bevis')	30–60cm (1–2ft)	Very intricately cut, lacy widespread fronds of mossy green

TOP TEN FERNS

 There are over 10,000 species to choose from. Even leaving out the tender kinds, there is a bewildering number. Picking the top ten is almost impossible, but might give us the following. They are deciduous or semi-evergreen unless stated.

MEDIUM FERNS

(30-60cm (1-2ft) tall)
Adiantum pedatum, American maidenhair
Asplenium scolopendrium, hart's tongue
Athyrium filix-femina, lady fern forms
Dryopteris erythrosorus, autumn fern
D. filix-mas in many forms, male fern
Onoclea sensibilis, sensitive fern
Polypodium vulgare, common polypody
Polystichum aculeatum forms, prickly shield fern
Polystichum setiferum in many forms, soft shield fern

COMPANION PLANTS FOR FERNS

Bergenia
Cyclamen
Galanthus, snowdrops
Helleborus argutifolius
H. foetidus
H. orientalis
Hosta
Iris species
Ligularia
Ornamental grasses
Smaller rhododendrons

JUNE

The longest days of the year run through this month and all plants
are in full growth. The spring is behind us, and with the
disappearance of the spring flowers the big battalions of summer
take over. Roses are coming into full bloom and in borders and
beds the oriental poppies, bearded irises and hybrid lilies are
making this a time of rich colour and splendour.

We think of this as a month of roses, and of course they appear to
be everywhere. But are they really as numerous as in years gone
by? It is certainly a time of high herbaceous endeavour: everything
seems to be in bloom or preparing to delight. The faded flowers of
spring have nearly all gone, and lupins with cathedral spires and
more lowly achilleas are in full flower.

The herbaceous plants may be accompanied by one or two bulbs.
Tulipa sprengeri *is the last tulip to bloom and may still be
displaying orange heads;* Camassia leichtlinii *carries its spikes of
bright blue. And here is* Galtonia candicans, *getting ready for its
later and long season of creamy bloom as the Cape hyacinth, at its
prime 60-90cm (2-3ft) tall. But there is one bulb that takes the
summer by storm. The lilies begin to show their splendour in early
summer and lead into high summer glory; the modern hybrids are
wonderful and very easy to grow.*

The shrubs that form the backbone of the garden at all times are
now very much in charge, in full leaf if not full bloom. Genistas
such as G.lydia *are a mass of gold;* Spiraea × vanhouttei *has its
many arching stems laden along their length with clusters of white
blossom; the long, weeping stems of* Buddleia alternifolia *are
wrapped around with scented, small lilac flowers. This is a
month to savour the garden at its most bountiful.*

tasks
FOR THE
month

PRUNE SPRING-FLOWERING SHRUBS

If this job has not already been completed, it should be finished early this month if you want to achieve the maximum display next spring. Cut flowered shoots back to 5-8cm (2-3in) from the main stem, leaving one or two buds to provide the new branch growth to carry next year's bloom. If you forget this pruning, however, do not worry: the shrubs will still put on a good display. After all, how many forsythias get a proper annual trim?

LOOKING AFTER CONTAINERS

Most containers will by now be in full growth and beginning to look good. With so much growth taking place, a lot of water will be lost through transpiration from the leaves and this needs replacing. Containers in open, breezy places will lose moisture more quickly and need checking more regularly.

As mentioned last month, the bigger the container the easier it is to look after and the bigger the possible reservoir of moisture and food.

Food should be provided by the slow-release fertilisers in the compost but, if necessary, extra fillips can be given via foliar feeding. There are plenty of proprietary foliar sprays available which are suitable for container-grown plants; just follow the instructions.

Where there are a large number of containers it may be worthwhile installing a trickle irrigation line, which will keep everything permanently moist. Most easy gardeners, however, will be content with just a few sizeable containers that they can manage with little effort; containers which sit on the ground or just above it are obviously the easiest to water and care for, and a few large ones that are well cared for will look far more impressive than a lot of smaller ones that are suffering. Try to include one or two good focal points in your garden.

BULBS

Foliage from dying daffodils can be removed six weeks after flowering if you need to bother. Tulip foliage can be removed rather more quickly after the blooms have faded, perhaps some three or four weeks; the leaves are certainly better removed if they begin to look tired or diseased.

By the middle of the month clumps of crowded daffodils can be lifted. For minimum trouble lift, split, remove damaged pieces and then replant the bulbs immediately, preferably in fresh stations giving them more room. Small pieces can

BULBS TO LIFT, SPLIT AND REPLANT

Daffodils
Tulips
Crocuses
Muscaris
Scillas
Snowdrops
Chiondoxas
Winter Aconites
Colchicums

WARNING

■ Label bulbs clearly and carefully at all times from lifting onwards: one bulb looks very much like another and getting them mixed up is very annoying. Almost all bulbs look best grown in groups of their own kind, so mixes are best avoided, especially the cheap ones offered at garden centres ■

be planted to fatten up and then bloom – or, if you already have too many, the tiddlers can be discarded or given away.

If the bulbs are to be stored they should be laid out in trays or open boxes in an airy, cool spot so that they can dry out before being roughly cleaned and stored in net bags, again in a cool, airy spot, until autumn planting. There may be a temptation to place the bulbs in the greenhouse to dry out, but this is not a good idea. The temperature can soar, and the bulbs will be scalded and badly damaged, if not killed.

MULCHING AND CONSERVING WATER

With summer upon us there may well be periods of drought. It is surprising how even in wet years there are times when water seems short, and naturally these coincide with hosepipe bans.

Mulches of shredded bark provide next to no feed, and indeed may hijack nitrogen-producing bacteria in the soil and create a temporary shortage, although some bagged bark comes with compensating fertiliser added. However, the invaluable labour-saving jobs that a 8-10cm (3-4in) layer of this mulch does are to:

■ inhibit weed seed germination and weed growth;

■ keep the soil cool;

■ maintain the topsoil in a receptive state to take in water from rainfall;

■ prevent the topsoil from drying out;

■ make all look neat and tidy.

Well-made compost used as a mulch will perform the same functions as the bark but, being a humus material, will also provide a steady source of nutrients.

The main loss of water in times of drought is through the leaves of plants, ie transpiration. Mulches help to conserve the soil moisture during the first few days of a drought, but the plants are still pumping water up through their roots and stems and into their leaves, where it is lost. Contrary to popular belief, the hoeing of topsoil hastens the loss of moisture as it breaks up the dried surface 'skin' which insulates the soil. Killing weeds by hoeing helps reduce the loss of water as the weeds are no longer taking up moisture, but this is best done when the weeds are in an early stage of growth and the ground is not completely dry. In hot, dry weather hoeing should stop. This is just what the easy gardener wants to hear!

Mulches are also very useful in the winter, when they prevent the soil freezing and help evergreens to continue taking in water to make good the loss by transpiration. Some of the worst effects of drought can be in a hard winter when the ground is badly frozen and high winds are pulling quantities of water from evergreen trees and shrubs.

MULCHES

Thoroughly rotted compost
Spent mushroom compost
Shredded bark
Gravel

(The above can all look well, the composts also providing food though the mushroom compost does contain lime)

Farmyard manure
Shredded hedge clippings
Sawdust
Spent hops

(These four are less attractive to the eye. Only the farmyard manure provides food. The others are efficient weed seed inhibitors)

HUMUS
Humus is a gel that attaches itself to particles in the soil, holding them together as crumbs. The gel retains water and allows the transfer of nutrient salts to the plant roots.

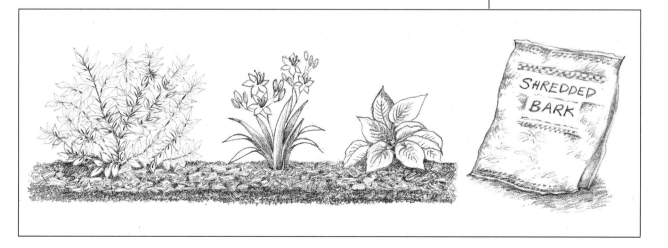

plants
OF THE
month

ROSES OF CHARACTER

'Ballerina'
Rosa banksia lutea ('Banksian
Yellow')
'Canary Bird'
'Celestial'
'Essex'
R. gallica versicolor (*Rosa mundi*)
'Mermaid'
R. moyesii 'Geranium'

ROSES TODAY

The great days of the rose garden as a feature of private gardens are past. Pure rose beds are being dug up: they spend too much of their time 'resting', out-of-work actors that look forlorn for many months through the winter. Rose beds can be underplanted with bulbs and other things, but this usually looks makeshift and not designed. Nowadays the rose has to perform several roles or work with a variety of other plants. 'Character' roses may climb walls, act as ground cover or occasionally perform a solo specimen act. Traditional bush (large-flowered) roses and floribundas now find themselves mixing in with a variety of herbaceous and shrubby plants – an unaccustomed egalitarian life, but they look well. Pruning is minimal with species, small and climbing roses. Floribundas can be simply cut to half their height in the winter. To avoid work pick cultivars recommended by growers as being disease resistant.

ROSA 'AMERICAN PILLAR'

ROSA 'KORRESIA'
(*'Freesia'*, *'Sunsprite'*)

type	Hardy shrub, floribunda rose. Bushy but erect
size	Height and spread 75cm (30in)
foliage	Dark, shiny, bold leaves
flowers	Clustered, largish yellow flowers, fully double, each 8cm (3in) across. Early summer into autumn.
site	As a spot plant in a border, grouped in a bed or used as an informal hedge
care	Strong and easy. Winter pruning to half height
other cultivars	Huge numbers including 'Ballerina', many clusters of small pink single flowers

ROSA 'AMERICAN PILLAR'

Climbing roses include kinds that reach well over 10m (30ft). Others, like 'American Pillar', are more useful lower down. This plant can be grown against a post or wall, or as a free-standing shrub.

type	Hardy rose, classified as a climber. Introduced 1908; a hybrid from (*R. wichuraiana* × *R. setigera*) × a red perpetual rose
size	Climbs to 3-4.5m (10-15ft)
foliage	Highly polished, good leaves. Spray to protect against mildew
flowers	Very profuse, with large bunches of rosy-carmine single flowers with a telling white eye. Makes a big impact for weeks from early summer
site	Needs room to display itself at the back of the border, by fences or near a wall
care	Strong grower and long lived. Old plants cut down to a stump will refurbish themselves quickly
propagation	By cuttings 15-25cm (6-8in), taken after leaf fall and inserted at least two thirds into gritty soil

ROSA 'LITTLE WHITE PET'

Some of the very tiny roses look delightful in pots waiting to be purchased, but can be a little disappointing in the garden. Not so 'Little White Pet', which spreads nicely and makes a pleasing plant.

ROSA WILSONII

type   Hardy, dwarf sport from the old climber 'Félicité et Perpétue'. Introduced 1879

size   Height 45cm (18in) but can spread to more than double the width

foliage   Dark, neat leaves

flowers   Very long season of crowded, single white blooms that almost completely hide the foliage, usually starting before the summer and lasting for months. Old and outstanding dwarf white kind, better and more lovable than a galaxy of kinds introduced in the past 12C years

site   In bed or border, perhaps falling over a retaining wall

care   Very hardy bush that will thrive without any pruning

propagation   By cuttings 10-15cm (4-6in), after leaf fall, or by layering in summer and leaving till spring

ROSA WILSONII

Owners of small gardens may find it hard to cope with some of the robust rose species, but if you can afford the space these are real character plants and breathtaking in bloom.

type   Hardy species making a wide thicket of strong, arching stems

size   Height 2-3m (6-10ft), at least twice as wide

foliage   Mid-green, healthy leaves

flowers   Covers the formidable bush in white, single flowers with golden bosses. Particularly good in early and midsummer

site   Towards the edge of the wild garden, the back of a large mixed shrubbery or as one of a screen of shrubs marking and making the boundary. Happy in most soils

propagation   By cuttings as for 'American Pillar'

care   Only choose this or a similar species if you have the room and are sure that you want to make it a permanent no-go area

ROSE SPECIES

R. glauca (rubrifolia), neat reddish leaves with a purple bloom, graceful habit, smallish pink flowers, attractive hips

R. moyesii, robust almost rampaging growth and heavily armed with thorns, but with deep, glowing red, wide single flowers and magnificent heavy crops of large, polished, brilliant red pendant hips

R. rugosa, disease-proof, attractive rough leaves and large single flowers, pink, red or white according to clone. What is thought of as the type plant of the species has rose-lilac blossom

J U N E

67

practical project

USING TRELLIS-WORK AND ARBOURS

TRELLIS-WORK

Trellis-work in the garden can be used in several ways. It is quick and easy to instal, providing the simplest method of immediate garden division. It can screen awkward or unsightly areas, provide support and shelter for plants, and can help to create the illusion of space and perhaps a sense of mystery. Standing alone it can be pleasing, and it may be the main component in constructing features such as arbours. In most gardens it will be called upon to fulfil several or all of these roles.

Wherever trellis is used it provides a barrier. It is not a completely impenetrable wall, but the eye is stopped and registers the screen and its height; the vertical vies with the horizontal. This begins to give the garden another dimension. The barrier stops the eye but it also begins to fascinate, and suggest extra space beyond. Even when trellis is fixed against a tall, blank wall, there is somehow the hovering feeling of further space, especially if the trellis is partially draped with climbing plants.

Designing with trellis-work

The long, narrow garden can make very good use of trellis. To the sides it can give extra height to walls or fences and provide support for climbers that will help to disguise the solidity of the walls and the uncompromising straightness of the boundaries. Some trellis at right angles to the long sides can jut part of the way into the precious space and halt the eye momentarily before it explores further. The narrowness of the garden can thus be masked and extra dimensions suggested.

The patio – so important in the easy garden – may need some extra privacy and shelter, and trellis-work can be an attractive and not too costly means of providing this. In the same manner, an arbour can be created with trellis in a suitably warm spot in the garden, with seating set on hardstanding and planted around with sweet-scented shrubs and flowers. This is the perfect place for the 'easy' gardener to relax and survey the garden from a new viewpoint.

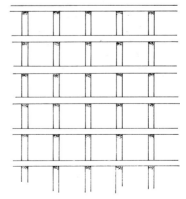

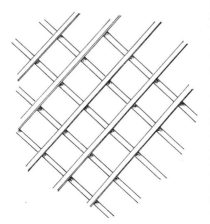

Choice of trellis-work

The choice is between 'rustic' and planed. Both types can be purchased in ready-made units, but the handyman/woman may find it a lot cheaper to buy the raw materials from a wood yard and make up his or her own. Rustic trellis made from 8-10cm (3-4in) thick poles, either round or half-round, should normally be stripped of bark and treated with preservative.

Shopping around will reveal a range of prices for the same goods. Usually sample structures are displayed and this will help you to visualise the effect in the garden and relate the heights and widths to the paths and to the human frame.

Construction

Trellis-work will provide considerable resistance to the wind, and this is greatly increased when it is clothed with climbing plants. It is therefore folly to skimp on the upright supports and their ground anchoring. Metal housing to take various sizes of posts are available; they are not cheap but, properly installed, will give you confidence in the strength of the structure. The alternative is to bed preservative-treated posts into holes that are then filled with concrete.

ARBOURS

A simple arbour can be arranged to the side of a pathway and will provide a retreat in which to sit and relax, but it also makes a focal point in the garden and gives it a touch of intimacy. The arbour is usually made to appear almost as a hideaway in a pleasing and secluded corner of the garden.

ERECTING TRELLIS

■ **Prop trellis in position and review appearance. Adjust position if necessary**

■ **Treat poles with wood preservative**

■ **Excavate holes to take bottom of poles to which trellis is attached. A 1.8m (6ft) trellis will need poles set 45cms (18in) into ground**

■ **Set poles into holes with concrete. Ensure concrete is flush with the surface and well worked into the base of the hole. Check that the pole is upright and in its exact position**

■ **Alternative anchoring can be provided by metal shoes. These need to be secured in the soil so that when the pole is housed in the shoe it is exactly vertical**

■ **Do not skimp the work of providing good anchorage. The trellis alone will catch the wind but when clothed by plants the force at times is going to be considerable. It is easier to make any extensive length of trellis stable if at least part of the ground support is at right angles**

plants
OF THE
month

HERBACEOUS PLANTS

Most herbaceous plants can be planted almost as permanently as shrubs. Even those traditionally recommended for annual lifting and splitting can usually be left three or four seasons. The list of trouble-free kinds include some that carry early summer-blooming into summer and autumn.

LONG-BLOOMING, TROUBLE-FREE PERENNIALS

Achillea 'Moonshine', yellow, summer
Anemone × hybrida cultivars, white, pink, late summer and autumn
Aster frikartii, purple mauve, midsummer into autumn
Campanula carpatica, blue, white, purple, summer
Coreopsis verticillata, gold, summer months
Euphorbia polychroma, limy yellow, all spring
E. characias wulfenii, limy yellow, all spring
Geranium endressii, pink, summer months
G. macrorrhizum, rich magenta, early and midsummer
G. 'Johnson's Blue', blue, summer
G. 'Russell Prichard', pink, summer

LIGULARIA PRZEWALSKII 'THE ROCKET'

LIGULARIA PRZEWALSKII, 'THE ROCKET'

All the ligularias in commerce are strong plants of extrovert character. They are at their best in damp or wet soils. The one chosen here is a splendid foliage and flowering plant.

type	Hardy, herbaceous, clump-forming perennial dying down for winter
size	Height 1.2-2m (4-6ft), spread, 1m (3ft). Taller in moist sites
foliage	Impressive round, leathery, serrated leaves of rich green with backs and stalks of dark, polished maroon. Few leaves on flower stems, these being deeply divided into narrow, pointed lobes
flowers	Tall, narrow spikes for long weeks in mid- to late summer. Very many small, deep golden daisies held on maroon-black erect stems
site	Good in full sun or part shade
soil	Enjoys moisture but can be grown in ordinary soils that do not dry to drought conditions
care	Strong, persistent. Plant early spring
propagation	Divide clumps in early autumn or early spring
other cultivars	*L. dentata* 'Desdemona', height 1.2m (4ft), spread 60cm (2ft), maroon green heart-shaped leaves and clusters orange daisies

KNIPHOFIA 'GOLD ELSE'

Red hot pokers are not by any means all red! There are lots of golden and lemon ones, as well as soft orange shades and bicolour orange or red and yellow. The range is from small kinds only 30cm (12in) high to the giants at 2m (6ft). Various cultivars open from late spring through to late autumn. Each is in bloom for a long time and plants can safely be left for several years with minimal attention.

type	Hardy perennial with fleshy rootstock
size	Height 1m (3ft), spread 60cm (2ft)
foliage	Long, folded, narrow leaves that bend over
flowers	Pure yellow, one of the first in early summer
planting	Plant in early autumn or early spring, allowing plenty of room
soil	Well drained, but it need not be over rich. Does well on poor soils
care	They enjoy being left alone. Cut away faded flower heads – you could encourage a second crop later
propagation	After three or more years clumps can be lifted and split. Take care not to lose too many of the long fleshy roots. Do this in early spring, ensuring that the roots are spread out in a large hole and that new plants are given the same soil

levels as before

other | 'Little Maid', pale cream, height
cultivars | 60cm (2ft), spread 45cm (18in); 'Royal Standard', orange and gold, height 1-1.2m (3-4ft), spread 60cm (2ft)

DORONICUM 'GOLD DWARF'

Daisy flowers are always attractive. The doronicums are all very easy plants; most are taller and later flowering than 'Gold Dwarf'. Other daisies like pink *Tanacetum* 'Eileen May Robinson' bloom now, but if cut back will give a small second crop in late summer.

type | Hardy, clump-forming perennial with strong, surface rhizomatous rootstock
size | Height 15-20cm (6-8in), spreads as clump to 60cm (2ft)
foliage | Light green, wide, heart-shaped, toothed leaves
flowers | Large yellow daisies freely produced in early spring. Opening a little later is a doubled form, 'Spring Beauty', with flowers almost like calendulas, 35-45cm (14-18in) tall in mid- and late spring
site | Open site with plenty of light. Give plants plenty of room
care | Easy plant with reasonable soil
propagation | Best divided every two or three years and older bits discarded

MISS WILMOTT'S GHOST
(*Eryngium giganteum*)

The common name commemorates a plantswoman of earlier this century who is reported as being in the habit of dropping seed of this plant in the gardens she visited.

type | Hardy biennial
size | Height 75cm-1.2m (30in-4ft), spread 60cm (2ft)
foliage | Forms a basal rosette of longish, heart-shaped leaves with serrations. Dark to mid-green and veined, in the first year. Some lobed leaves appear on flowering stems in the second year
flowers | Much-branched, wide heads of silver flower cones backed by vividly silvered, savagely pointed bracts. Very persistent in bloom from midsummer. Produces lots of seed and aged seedheads are still decorative in early winter, when they have become fawny grey

site | Allow plenty of room in an open, light site
soil | Reasonably fertile
propagation | Normally biennial, the large quantities of seed produced means that left alone there are likely to be thousands too many seedlings. Hoe through the surplus, and perhaps transfer a few small ones to new sites

ORIENTAL POPPIES
(*Papaver orientale*)

type | Hardy perennial with strong, fleshy rootstock
size | Height and spread 40-75cm (16-30in)
foliage | Rough, hairy, grey-green toothed and divided, spear-shaped leaves
flowers | Many large glossy petalled blooms, usually with a dark central blotch. Impressive boss of anthers around large ovary
planting | Plant in well-drained soil
site | Open, sunny spot
soil | Best in poor soils
care | Cut back leaves and stems after flowering to keep tidy and allow fresh leaves to take possession of the site
propagation | By root cuttings or by dividing clumps
cultivars | 'Perry's White', white with purple centre; 'Mrs Perry', salmon pink; 'May Queen', orange; 'Indian Chief', red

PAPAVER ORIENTALE 'MRS PERRY'

LONG-BLOOMING, TROUBLE-FREE PERENNIALS

Kniphofia, cream, yellow, orange, red, early summer to mid-autumn
Ligularia, yellow, summer
Lupins, various colours, early and midsummer
Nepeta 'Six Hills Giant', purple-blue, summer
Paeonies, white, pink, red, late spring to midsummer
Rudbeckia fulgida 'Goldsturm', gold, late summer to late autumn

PERENNIALS FOR DRY SHADE

Acanthus spinosus, bear's breeches
Alchemilla mollis, lady's mantle
Brunnera macrophylla, Siberian bugloss
Euphorbia robbiae, wood spurge
Iris foetidissima, stinking iris
Lamium, dead nettle
Polygonatum, Solomon's seal
Polygonum affine, dwarf knotweed
Tiarella cordifolia, foamflower
Vinca, periwinkle

PERENNIALS FOR DAMP SOILS

Astilbe
Astrantia, masterwort
Caltha palustris, kingcup, marsh marigold
C.p. 'Flore Pleno', double kingcup
Filipendula palmata 'Elegantissima', form of meadowsweet
F. purpurea
F. ulmaria aurea, golden-leaved meadowsweet
Iris ensata (I.kaempferi), Japanese flag
Iris sibirica, Siberian flag
Rodgersia aesculifolia, chestnut-leaved rodgersia
R.pinnata
R.podophylla
R.sambucifolia
Trollius, globe flower

J U N E

practical project

GROWING HEDGES AND SCREENS

RECOMMENDED HEDGING PLANTS

Berberis stenophylla, evergreen
Carpinus betulus, hornbeam
Fagus sylvatica, beech
F.s. purpurea, purple beech
Ilex aquifolium, hollies in variety
***Prunus cerasifera* 'Pissardii',** purple-leaved cherry plum

Hornbeam and beech, kept trimmed, will retain their dead leaves as a rusty brown dress for winter.

We use hedges and screens to mark boundaries, and to give privacy and shelter to the garden. They can provide a pleasing edging to the domain, like a frame around a picture. Within the garden lesser hedges may be planted as part of the design, to mark out one part of the garden from another, or perhaps to protect a bed of special plants.

WORKING WITH HEDGES

Long hedges will always require work. Even the slower-growing kinds will need trimming at least once or twice a year. With modern electric hedgetrimmers the job may be less daunting, but you will certainly need to 'budget' carefully for the amount of work you are letting yourself in for when you plant a quick-growing

WARNING

■ *Very fine impenetrable hedges can be made of holly or yew, which have the advantage of being evergreen and richly coloured. However, yew is poisonous to stock and is to be avoided next to farm fields. The fastest-growing conifer of all is × Cupressocyparis leylandii but it easily gets too tall if not constantly cut back, making for a lot of work. A selection of good hedging plants is given in the margin* ■

hedge such as Leyland cypress or privet.

Another drawback to long hedges is that some hedging plants can be very greedy and send out a mass of fibrous root through the topsoil for several feet. You may wish to use this space for other purposes, so you will need to take preventive measures. When you open up the trench in which to plant your hedge, line the garden side of it with heavy-grade polythene to stop exploration into the garden. Such a barrier would need to be about 45-60cm (18in-2ft) deep to be effective against most strong, surface-rooting hedge plants.

SCREENS – AN EASIER ALTERNATIVE

Hedges are usually clipped neatly and kept to a regular shape: they are living walls. They can look very fine, but why not make life easier? Alternative screens could be made of trellis with plants growing through it (see p.68) or could consist of shrubs and/or trees grown for similar purposes as a hedge but not kept formally clipped.

If you are looking for a decorative boundary or barrier that does not demand a lot of work, there are several reasons for growing screens rather than hedges. If shrubs and trees are grouped or lined up less formally than a hedge, you will not need to spend hours clipping the screen and then the same amount of time again carting away the clippings. A screen can consist of several or many different species; it can include both evergreens and deciduous types, and you will be able to enjoy shows of different

Carpinus betulus 'Fastigiata'

Ilex

blossom and perhaps autumn colour. The variety will make the screen very much more part of the garden than a hedge, and will probably make the garden look larger.

Trees can be included in the screen, as can all sizes of shrubby plants right down to small heathers. The screen can become more of a shrubbery, a planting that melts into the landscape or effectively hides unsightly views.

Planting a screen

The best time to plant is autumn, but with container-grown plants it could be tackled at almost any time except in the middle of a heatwave. Choose a selection of trees and shrubs from the lists in the margin to create an effective and decorative screen. Each specimen must be firmly planted in well dug soil in a hole that is as deep as the pot. A screen looks best with a staggered series of sites, taking care that each kind has plenty of room for its expected growth.

Acer campestre

*Prunus subhirtella
'Autumnalis'*

RECOMMENDED SCREENING PLANTS

TREES
Acer campestre, field maple
***Carpinus betulus* 'Fastigiata',** fastigiate hornbeam
***Fagus sylvatica* 'Dawyck',** fastigiate beech
***F.s.* 'Dawyck Gold',** fastigiate, golden leaves
***F.s.* 'Dawyck Purple',** fastigiate, purple leaves
Ilex, hollies in variety
***Prunus* 'Amanogawa',** upright pink-flowered cherry
***Prunus subhirtella* 'Autumnalis',** winter-flowering cherry

SHRUBS
***Berberis thunbergii* 'Atropurpurea',** deciduous, purple-red leaves
Cotoneaster franchetii, widespread branches, orange berries
C. lacteus, robust semi-evergreen, dark red berries
C. simonsii, strong-growing, upright, bright orange berries
***C. watereri* 'Cornubia',** large shrub/small tree, persistent red berries
Escallonia macrantha and cultivars, evergreen, white, pink or red blossom
***Ligustrum ovalifolium* 'Aureum',** golden privet
Prunus cistena, upright shrub, pink flowers
Pyracantha in variety, evergreen, yellow, orange or red berries

Roses in variety including:
***Rosa* 'Fru Dagmar Hastrop',** single flesh pink, veined flowers
R. glauca, graceful with small purple-red foliage and rosy-red flowers
R. rugosa, dense bushes, attractive large foliage, flowers white, pink or red
R. wilsonii, hugely robust, impenetrable shrub, masses of white blossom

JULY

This month is sunshine, deep blue skies and lush growth. High summer, and garden visiting gets into full swing; herbaceous borders and summer shrubs are critically examined and admired, ideas (and plants) are carried away to be tried out at home. Roses are now in full dress; the popular clematis are bedecking walls and trellis as well as clambering over shrubs and trees. Lilies are spectacular, as only lilies can be, now that the hugely scented trumpet kinds are loading the air with fragrance. The water garden is at its best; with bright skies the water looks colourful, reflecting the sky and the wonderful growth around the margins, while supporting the pads and flowers of lovely water-lilies. It is a great time for garden lovers.

Even those gardens whose best time is the spring may be enjoyed for their design and their foliage. Now we can see why we should look to foliage rather than always flowers when we go picking and choosing in the garden centres. A plant may carry flowers for a few days or weeks, but it keeps its foliage for many months, if not all year round. Ferns, ultimate foliage plants, can be at their best, fully grown but still fresh and without gale damage or any wear. They need no flowers to gild their beauty.

We should be enjoying sitting outside this month, and perhaps also eating there. On the patio we can admire the nearby beds, the climbers scrambling up and over the trellis; we see the garden as a whole and the colourful containers close by. These may be troughs filled with a collection of alpines, or jardinères holding lilies or geraniums (pelargoniums) in a riot of colour. As effective as anything amongst all the floral excitement at high summer may be an occasional large container boasting the calm presence of a substantial shrub or small tree.

tasks

FOR THE

month

ROSES
Cutting off dead flowers makes the bushes look tidy. If you prune back to the first full leaf, repeat-flowering kinds will quickly start producing wood for later flowers. Rambling and climbing roses can be pruned by removing weak flowered stems to encourage fresh growth for next year.

CHECKLIST

☐ Propagate trees and shrubs by air layering
☐ Divide bearded irises
☐ Propagate shrubs and some herbaceous plants by softwood cuttings
☐ Water plants in beds and borders in very dry periods

AIR LAYERING

Simple, reliable and quick to do, air layering is an ideal way to propagate almost any shrub or tree. If you can get a twig to bend down to soil level, peg it there and cover it with soil, you need not even bother with air layering, but often it is not so easy to pull branches down to ground level.

Getting a shoot to form roots whilst still a part of the parent plant has several benefits: the shoot is still being nourished naturally; it does not need watering or fussing over; it is safe and can be left for as long as necessary to root without worry.

■ Select a young shoot around 23-30cm (9-12in) long.

■ Remove a few of the leaves so that there is sufficient room to work.

■ Using a sharp knife, either graze a 5cm (2in) length of the leafless portion or cut a third or half-way into the shoot and create a tongue, working towards the tip of the shoot.

■ Dust the grazed or cut portion with hormone rooting powder.

■ Either wrap this worked length with moist sphagnum moss, with a little tucked in to keep the tongue open, or, using some plastic sheeting approximately 30cm (12in) square and waterproof tape, enclose the cut length with one or two handfuls of moist peat or compost. In this case, ensure that the plastic bandage makes a tight fit at both ends, so that the layer will be kept moist but will not be flooded by rain.

■ Summer layers of many shrubs will be robustly rooted by autumn leaf fall and can then be potted up and grown on. More vigorous types can be planted out in the spring. Some subjects will take longer to root; simply unwrap every so often and check progress.

DIVIDING BEARDED IRISES

Established clumps of bearded irises are best propagated immediately after blooming. New rhizomes can be snapped off from old worn-out ones that are then discarded. Cut the foliage back by half so that the new plants are less likely to be rocked by wind. New rhizomes should be anchored as firmly as possible but with the rhizome tops left exposed to the sun. These irises need good drainage and sunshine, but are otherwise very easy and rewarding plants.

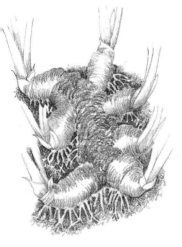

TAKING SOFTWOOD CUTTINGS

Lots of shrubs and other plants can be increased easily to fill up the garden by taking cuttings of shoots before they become woody.

■ Shrub cuttings 5-8cm (2-3in) long with two leaves or part leaves left on will normally be quite adequate.

■ Using a sharp knife, cut cleanly at a leaf axil (the node) where the stem is fractionally stronger.

■ Dip the cutting into hormone rooting powder and insert it firmly into a rooting medium of gritty compost, a mix of peat and grit, or a sandframe.

■ Keep moist and cover with glass or plastic to restrict loss of moisture through transpiration.

■ Rooting should be underway in a few weeks, at which stage the cuttings can be carefully potted up, and cared for by being protected from wind and not allowed to dry out.

Some herbaceous plants, such as all sorts of pinks, can be increased easily by taking 'pips' – cuttings from the growing points. Cutting size depends on the cultivar but is usually only 4-5cm (1½-2in).

IRRIGATION

When watering, do this well so that the first few inches of soil are thoroughly soaked – do not be deceived by the wet surface appearance. It is better by far, and less work, to restrict yourself to one or two substantial soaks in summer than to be spraying around with a hosepipe almost every day.

Getting water exactly where you need it can be achieved by using trickle irrigation units. These are pipes with small nozzles embedded in them and can be attached to a hosepipe or tap. The pipes are then laid so that the nozzles are close to the plants to be watered and the tap is turned on far enough for water to drip from each nozzle. The water percolates downwards and widely. None is wasted being evaporated from the surface as with spray lines.

WEEDS

■ *If possible run a hoe over open soil between plants before going on holiday. This should ensure that germinating weed seed is inhibited and that your return is not met with a strong crop of weeds. Grounsel, chickweed, grasses, speedwell and other annuals can soon take over unhoed parts if there is sufficient seed in the soil* ■

SOME PLANTS TO PROPAGATE FROM SOFTWOOD CUTTINGS

Abelia
Arbutus
Artemisia
Aster (Michaelmas daisy)
Aubrieta
Aucuba
Brachyglottis (Senecio)
Calamintha
Ceanothus
Choisya
Chrysanthemum
Cistus
Clematis
Columnea
Corylopsis
Crassula
Dahlia
Delphinium
Erigeron
Escallonia
Euonymus
Gentiana
Gypsophila
Hebe
Hop
Hydrangea
Hypericum
Jasminum
Lamium
Lavendula
Lavatera
Linum
Lupin
Mimulus
Monarda
Pelargonium (Geranium)
Penstemon
Philadelphus
Potentilla
Pyracantha
Rosemary
Salvia
Santolina
Saxifraga
Scabiosa
Sedum
Teucrium
Thymus
Verbena
Vinca
Vitis (vine)

plants
OF THE
month

EASY LILIES
The lilies most frequently on sale in garden centres are the early and midsummer-flowering Asiatic hybrids. Probably the easiest of all lilies, the range now is very wide, and all are worth trying. They are splendid border plants and wonderful in pots.

EASY ASIATIC LILY HYBRIDS

'Alpine Glow', blush pink
'Grand Cru', gold with mahogany centre
'Mercedes', brilliant deep red
'Mont Blanc', cream white
'Roma', white
'Sterling Star', white, with dark spots
'Yellow Blaze', gold with few freckles

LILIES

Summer is lily time. The first wave are the Asiatic hybrids, such as 'Enchantment', which started flowering last month. Hot on their heels come the trumpets such as L. regale and for some weeks they overlap. The trumpets are still sounding their silent music and spilling perfume around when the later gorgeous Oriental hybrids open, kinds such as the popular cut flower 'Stargazer'.

Plant all the bulbs in early autumn or early spring with good drainage but with at least 10-15cm (4-6in) of soil over their tops. The kinds listed below will tolerate some lime but do enjoy an open soil with enough humus to give it a slightly acid flavour.

LILIUM 'ENCHANTMENT'

type	Hardy, concentric bulb of incurving scales. Asiatic hybrid
size	First-year bulbs can reach 75cm (30in) at flowering, but older plants may grow to 1.2m (4ft)
foliage	Well furnished with mid-green, polished, long eliptical leaves
flowers	Upright-facing, crowded heads of long-petalled, flaming orange flowers dotted dark maroon-black
site	Open or semi-shaded spots outside or in pots/containers
soil	Best in well-drained, open soil with plenty of leafy humus

LILIUM REGALE

care	Remarkably robust. After two years in late summer dig up, split bulbs and replant, giving each more space
propagation	Apart from division, increase is by the small bulbs formed on the stem below ground and bulbils that may appear in the leaf axils. (Cutting off the flowerheads when in bud will usually induce the production of masses of bulbils. This works with many Asiatic hybrids.) Bulbs can also be increased by scales, see 'African Queen'

REGAL LILY
(*Lilium regale*)

type	Hardy, large, concentric bulb with scales. Trumpet species
size	Height at flowering 50cm-2m (20in-6ft). Good newly planted bulbs grow to 60-90cm (2-3ft), but taller after the first year
foliage	Many narrow, dark green leaves up the stem
flowers	From the single bloom of a small seedling bulb to over two dozen large, outward-facing trumpets on mature bulbs. Buds pinky and maroon, open blooms snow white with a rich golden base. Petals 12-15cm (5-6in) long. Highly fragrant
site	Open, sunny spot, perhaps between shrubs or herbaceous plants so that, like most lilies, it can enjoy shade at its toes but have its face in the sun. Splendid in large containers
soil	Grows well in a wide variety of soils, but probably best in humus-rich, gritty, well-drained soils or composts
care	Very strong-growing, easy species thoroughly recommended for beginners, but everyone loves it
propagation	By division, scales or from seed. Plants can be flowering in two years from seed
varieties	Pure white forms are sold as *L. regale album*

LILIUM 'AFRICAN QUEEN'

type	Hardy, large, concentric bulb with bulky scales. Trumpet hybrid
size	Height at flowering 1.2-2m (4-6ft)

foliage Dark-green, long, pointed narrow leaves scattered up the stem

flowers Massive flared trumpets of glowing deep orange; buds dark – almost chocolate brown. From one to three dozen on a stem. Richly perfumed

site Open site with drainage

soil Enjoys deep, open soils with plenty of humus

care Strong grower

propagation By division or scales. Break off scales cleanly as close as possible to the basal plate, dip in fungicide and insert the severed edge downwards in an equal mix of peat and grit. This operation can take place in spring or summer. Kept moist in a plastic-covered tray, small bulbils will form after a few weeks. These can be potted on and later planted out to grow into flowering bulbs

LILIUM 'LIBERATION'

type Hardy, concentric bulb with tightly clasped scales. Asiatic hybrid

size Height at flowering 75cm-1m (2½-3ft)

foliage Plenty of shiny, rich green upward- and outward-reaching, narrow pointed leaves

flowers Many flowers crowded into pyramidal heads, facing outwards and upwards. Very rich pink

site Between shrubs or herbaceous plants in a sunny or semi-shaded bed

soil Well drained

care Clumps can be split every two or three years to prevent overcrowding

propagation By division or scales

LILIUM 'CONNECTICUT KING'

type Hardy, concentric bulb of strong, incurved white scales. Asiatic hybrid

size Height at flowering 1m (3ft)

foliage Flat, highly polished, rich green leaves freely produced on strong stems

flowers Plenty of wide-petalled, upward-facing, deep golden-yellow blooms with rather richer centres but without spots

site Open area

soil Well drained

care Very strong grower. Split clumps every two years

propagation Many bulbs form on the stems below ground. Bulbils will probably also be found in some leaf axils. These can be grown on in trays for a few months before planting out, or plant out straightaway into open, leafy soil

LILIUM 'LIBERATION'

POTTED LILIES
Lilies are the easiest of all bulbs to grow in pots. A 20cm (8in) pot will take three or five bulbs, depending on size. Place a little humus-rich compost in the pot and set the bulbs in as low as possible. Fill the pot with compost. In a conservatory or cold greenhouse, bulbs planted in early spring will be in bloom in fourteen weeks. Ericaceous compost will serve lilies well.

practical project

USING WALLS IN THE GARDEN

PLANTS FOR WALL CREVICES

Arabis, white or pink, spring
Aubrieta, various colours, spring
Campanula, blue, purple or white, spring and summer
Erigeron mucronatus, white and pink daisies, spring to autumn
Helianthemum (rock rose) various colours, summer
Iberis sempervirens, white, spring
Lewisia, various colours, spring
Lithodora diffusa, blue, all summer
Polygonum affine, pink, all summer
Saxifraga, various colours, mainly spring
Sedum, plants with flowers in summer
Sempervivum, foliage plants with flowers in summer

PURPOSES AND FORMS

Garden walls have several roles, and in some positions one role takes precedence over others.

Boundary walls mark the limits of the property and garden, provide barriers and give shelter. Interior walls may be used to hold back soil and form terracing on a sloping site, contain soil as raised beds, or can be used to define parts of the garden and be themselves a decorative as well as a utilitarian part of the overall design.

The aesthetic value of the walls themselves is important. They provide a vertical as well as a horizontal element to the garden design, the eye hitting the wall as a barrier or plane in opposition to the usual dominant horizontal one. They provide solidity, texture and colour to define parts of the garden and provide a background setting for the plants. They ought to look good, and be as easy to construct and as maintenance free as possible.

MATERIALS

The use of a lot of very different materials in the garden infrastructure can shatter any sense of unity and peace. However, the bold use of two of three contrasting kinds can be very effective and provide a lively setting for the plants – most types of stone and brick are friendly to plants in this way.

Railway sleepers
These can be the easy gardener's regular stand-by when dealing with construction projects; they are very useful for creating quick, low walls. Each is 2.5m (8ft) long and can be handled easily by two fit people. In fact, they are not impossibly difficult for one person to manipulate once they have been carried to the working site. See the practical project on p84-5 for details on their use.

Bricks, blocks and stone
Ease of handling, appearance and cost are the main factors governing choice. Red or orange brick looks pleasing and may provide some unity with the house. Yellow and blue bricks can feel more at odds with the growing plants, but can sometimes be used to provide a strong contrast. Bricks should be frost proof, and their uniformity makes them easy to handle. The only easier materials will be prefabricated, decorative cement blocks, often 30cm (1ft) square, or breeze blocks.

Whilst breeze blocks may seem an ugly, utilitarian material, they can be used for low walls when treated to allow extensive moss growth and then allowed to become overgrown with clambering plants – a cheap and easy interior wall can be made quickly using breeze blocks that are then overgrown with some of the attractive variegated ivies.

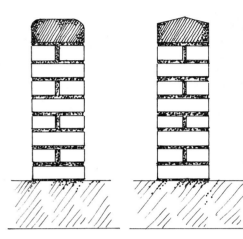

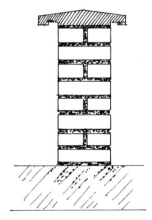

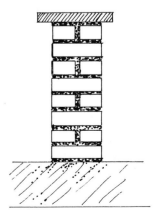

Solid concrete prefabricated blocks can be bought in two thicknesses, 115mm and 235mm (4½in and 9in). For a substantial wall you could use the hollow kind which measure 235mm × 235mm × 450mm (9in × 9in × 18in). With neat coping stones, a smart effect can be achieved when the whole neatly cemented wall is finished off with paint, which it takes easily. In the right place such a wall, which can be straight or curved, can look very architectural and impressive – certainly a good backcloth for shrubs and climbers.

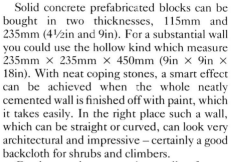

Good natural stone makes walls of great character but, unless there is a reasonable local supply, stone can be incredibly expensive. Reconstituted stone may be an option; it is produced in even, easily handled sizes and soon loses its initial rather too new appearance.

DRY VERSUS BONDED

Important boundary walls will be bonded or, in some rural situations, be substantial dry stone walls. They will necessarily have to be strong. Inside the garden the decorative value of the wall can be more important.

Dry walls

A dry wall of stone may allow for the growing of plants within it, particularly when double walls are built with soil in between. Dry containing walls used against banks or for terracing are also valuable homes for plants. Any such dry walls need their stability ensured by providing firm foundations and laying each course so that it tends to exert pressure inwards rather than slipping out. To underpin this security, dry walls are best given a 'batter', leaning at least 5° inwards from the vertical. An occasional larger stone leaning further back into the bank will be an added guarantee of stability.

Dry walls need not be *completely* dry. For ease of construction and greater stability, a trowelful of mortar can be added behind the join of each pair of rocks. The outer appearance remains that of a dry stone wall.

Bonded walls

Brick-built walls should be either 11.5cm or 23cm (4½ or 9in) wide. The thicker walls are not only stronger but look more visually correct, especially if finished off with a coping layer of bricks set on edge. An alternative finish will be precast concrete copings which look smart and are laid more quickly.

If a long exterior wall is being built it is wise to allow for the natural expansion and contraction caused by varying temperatures, thus forestalling the likelihood of cracks appearing.

A decorative way of doing this is to stagger the wall so that you have natural breaks every so often. You can even turn the wall at right angles for a section and provide a cosy corner for some favoured plants.

DESIGN PRINCIPLES

Remember that a guiding principle of good design is simplicity. Do not allow any of your planning and building to become too fussy and intricate. Walls are for utility and decoration but they are also framework parts of the design; it is the garden within that is our main concern. The contrasts between the living plant and the inanimate constructions can be important factors in the design. The walls give us boundaries, design masses and lines, backgrounds for our plants and shelter for both plants and ourselves.

The taller the wall or fence the greater the pressure that gale-force winds can exert upon it: sound foundations and maybe buttressing will help. You might like to try a honeycomb wall. Being able to see through invites exploration, awakening an interest in what is beyond.

plants
OF THE
month

HOSTAS

Hostas have been fashionable for quite some time, and huge numbers of novelties are being bred. There will be a swing of fashion against them soon – do not take any notice, they are marvellous foliage plants!

You could do worse than plant some of the old kinds with a few of the newer ones. The latest novelty can be surprisingly expensive and may not be that much better than established kinds. The following are widely available:

Hosta fortunei albopicta, pale yellow

H. 'Francee', rich green, broad white margins

H. 'Halcyon', neat blue-green

H. sieboldiana, huge blue-green leaves

H. 'Zounds', yellow, somewhat olive later

OTHER FOLIAGE PLANTS
There are too many outstanding foliage plants to list here. Some are highlighted in the various lists and descriptions of shrubs through the book and in Appendix 2, but it would be a mistake not to consider the value of two other groups: the ferns and the ornamental grasses. Both can be used to very good effect in many sites and especially some awkward ones – ferns in very shady areas and some grasses where little else will thrive.

FOLIAGE PLANTS

Flowers last days or perhaps a week or two, but foliage is with us most of the time. We should look to the foliage first when buying plants, along with the general character of the plant; blossom is then a bonus. The choice is tremendously wide: there is colour, size, texture, shape and even scent to take into consideration, as well as the form of the plants and their habits.

PHOTINIA 'RED ROBIN'

type	Hardy, evergreen shrub
size	Height 6m (20ft), spread 3.5m (12ft), but can be pruned to suit
foliage	Strong, oblong, unserrated leaves of a rich dark green, but young foliage is a vivid red and this colour is held for an extraordinary number of weeks or months before slowly taking on the handsome polished adult green
flowers	Wide heads of small, white, five-petalled flowers in late spring. These are not unattractive but the foliage is the main attraction – brighter than many shrub flowers
site	Sun or semi-shade
soil	Enjoys deep good soil
care	Straightforward and frost hardy, best out of driving wind
cultivars	'Birmingham', very similar

PHOTINIA 'RED ROBIN'

MACLEAYA CORDATA

PLUME POPPY
(Macleaya cordata)

type	Hardy, herbaceous perennial with vigorous, suckering rootstock. A member of the poppy family, but you would not immediately guess this
size	Height 1.5m (5ft). Suckering spread can quickly make a 2m (6ft) stand
foliage	Magnificent large, rounded leaves with fairly deep, rounded indentations, a lovely grey-green above and almost white below and held from the milk-white stems on white stalks. The white colouring has a hint of pink beneath. Leaves get smaller the higher up the stem they are
flowers	In summer the stems are topped by branched heads of panicles of tiny white flowers that are made to look like a coral-coloured haze by the bracts and stems
site	Very easy in full sun
soil	Well drained; will manage in some poorer sites
care	Spreads rapidly, so needs positioning with some foresight, perhaps best at the back of the border or in the middle of a large bed where it can make a very strong focal point. The main

concern will be to contain the spread

propagation By division in early spring or strong root cuttings in winter

HOSTA 'ZOUNDS'

The hostas are immensely popular, but do not let this put you off – most popular things earn their status, and hostas are foliage plants *par excellence*. Many novelties are now being bred, especially in America, and introduced all over the world.

type Hardy, herbaceous perennial with strong, fibrous rootstock

size Height 30cm (1ft), larger in damp, rich soils; Spread 60-90cm (2-3ft)

foliage Impressive, large, wide leaves of gold, fading just a touch with age but always eyecatching

flowers Pale lilac, nodding, long bells in midsummer

soil Enjoys good deep soil that is moist but drained

site Can be grown in open sites, but perhaps at its very best in coolish semi-shade

care Slug and snail deterrents are useful, especially in early spring. Keep the soil clean around the plants

propagation By division in early spring

other cultivars See margin

 ## *ACTINIDIA KOLOMIKTA*

type Hardy, deciduous climber with twining stems

size Height 3.5m (12ft)

foliage Oval, heart shaped, 8-15cm (3-6in) long and up to 8cm (3in) wide. Starting somewhat purplish in youth, the leaves become mid-green but with many more or less white and/or pink. Sometimes this colour only paints the tips, but half leaf cover is frequent and a good scattering are fully given over to these bright, unusual colourings. Very splendid from spring through to late summer

flowers Small, white, scented flowers in summer, one sex to a plant

site Best on a wall with strong trellis support, sun or shade

soil Enjoys soil in good heart

care Do not allow to dry out at the roots

propagation By semi-ripe cuttings in midsummer, or by air-layering

ACTINIDIA KOLOMIKTA

practical project

RAISED BEDS AND TERRACING

PLANTING UP DRY BANKS
Where banks are sharply drained and inclined to dry out, the shrubs should be chosen to withstand this. In sunny spots you could plant Brachyglottis *(Senecio) 'Sunshine' with its silver-grey foliage and yellow daisy flowers, together with lots of brooms and cistuses. Heathers, too, will help to provide dense ground cover to cut down on weed problems. Silver-leaved artemsias and santolinas will also look cheerful. There are low growing ground-cover roses and cotoneasters too.*

RAISED BEDS

Raised beds have several advantages. They can make a definite feature in the garden design and give better drainage to the resident plants. The extra height and the retaining walls provide sites which will show off some plants to advantage, especially those that are never happier than when cascading over and down a wall. More practically, the plants will be closer to the eye to admire and to the hand to tend, saving a great deal of bending and potential backache for the gardener. See the practical project on p80-1 for details on the choice of walling materials and construction.

TERRACING

Gardeners with flat ground yearn for interesting undulations, those with sloping ground want the more easily managed flat areas. Sloping ground does give opportunities for creating a managed landscape by terracing which, once completed, is usually easy to look after and can display plants of all kinds very much more dramatically than on the flat.

Full-scale terracing ends with the fall of ground contained within walls, so that the combined height of all the walls is the same as the total fall of the ground, with the terraces themselves level.

Planted slopes – a simple answer

An easier and less expensive alternative is simply to engineer some pathways and then plant up the slope with shrubs and trees; rela-

tively few hours of work with a spade and rake will provide you with the basis for reasonable pathways. Paths can be simply made of shredded bark; it looks natural and inhibits weed growth. Grass banks will involve continual and difficult maintenance problems and are to be avoided. See the margin for suggested plants for dry banks.

Constructing terraces

The walls of terraces can be a major feature if the ground loses considerble height and substantial walls have to be built. Great opportunities are thus provided for growing interesting plants that need a wall for support or warmth. Even modest slopes can be used to incorporate some steps, a feature that can be a lasting pleasure and focal point if well designed and constructed. It is sensible, however, to think about whether it will be easier to negotiate your particular slope when wheeling a barrow or mower than to pull machinery up and down steps (this will mean leaving or creating a reasonably even slope). Remember, though, that the eye is a very fallible instrument when gauging degrees of slope, so always use a spirit level when undertaking any work – the fall in levels is almost always far more than you calculated by eye.

On very sloping ground over a considerable distance it may be necessary to build more than one terrace, and then if steps are incorporated it may be best to have them placed so that you climb one set and then walk along a terrace path before reaching the next.

■ *Railway sleepers*
A quick wall can be built using railway sleepers. If a level base is prepared, their own weight will usually ensure that they do not move. They should be laid bolt holes downwards so that these do not provide a place for water to gather and begin rotting the wood, though this is not usually too much of a problem as they are heavily impregnated with tar. Sleepers measure 2.5m × 20cm × 12cm (8ft × 8in × 5in). They are long lasting and can look effective, especially when plants are growing around and partially over them. They are particularly useful when there is about 30cm (1ft) of rising ground to be contained; here, a second row of sleepers on top of the first will suffice. Containing a greater depth of soil will probably be better managed using brick or stone.

■ *Brick and stone*
Brick or stone walls need to be built securely and represent a considerable investment.

Make sure that the materials to be used are absolutely weatherproof; being in contact with moist or wet soil all their life and repeatedly frosted will cause stresses that will result in poor materials shattering.

Colour is important. Blue engineering bricks are tremendously weather resistant but can be a little 'cold' in appearance, though they look smart and may be exactly what you need to contrast with shrubs or plants of flamboyant shapes and/or colours. Red bricks for walls are 'warm' and a friendly contrast to the greenery.

Whether the walls are bonded with mortar or are dry (see p81), they should have firm foundations. Used for terraces, there will be constant moisture and sometimes a lot of water gathering behind; the inner brick surfaces can be waterproofed before being laid, but the more important factor is to allow for water drainage. Leave small gaps low down in the wall approximately every metre (yard) to allow water to run away. This is imperative with bonded walls, and it is often best to arrange this on the second course, which helps to lessen the possibility of soil being washed out with the water.

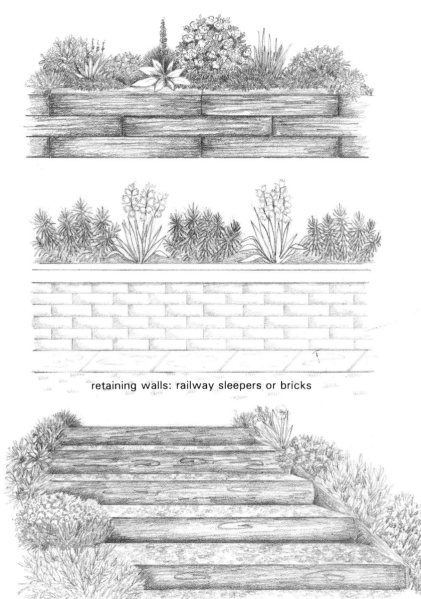

retaining walls: railway sleepers or bricks

steps of logs and gravel

PLANTING TERRACES

Terraces can be ideal homes for a wide range of shrubs, bold herbaceous plants and bulbs. The alpine enthusiast may see a terrace as just the place for his alpines. Sharp drainage can be as good as pure scree conditions. For visual impact from a distance a collection of shrubs will be very effective and virtually trouble free. Shrub roses and some of the species could be used to very good effect, concentrating on kinds that need little or no pruning. If more variety is needed the shrubs can be interplanted with bold herbaceous plants (see margin).

STEPS

Steps are 'speaking' parts of the garden design; they say 'Come this way'. They certainly invite you to explore further or to return to base camp. Near the house, more formal steps of brick or faced stone will seem right; leading through a bank of trees a less formal manner is appropriate, and logs held in position by strong wedges driven into the ground can look right. Behind each log the step will be made of a fast-draining mix, with a surface of chippings or shredded bark.

Railway sleepers sawn to appropriate widths

make good risers for steps. They should be backfilled with hardcore topped with chippings, bricks or slabs. The steps may run straight up, but in certain places could be more pleasing and informal if they turn through an angle of anything from 20° to 45°.

Height of steps should not exceed 20cm (8in). Lesser heights can look more pleasing, while for comfort and appearance the steps themselves should be deep, perhaps not less than 60cm (2ft).

PERENNIALS FOR TERRACES
Interplant shrubs on terraces with perennials such as dwarf delphiniums, lupins, paeonies, ligularias, rudbeckias, the bolder geraniums and late summer Anemone × hybrida *cultivars.*

AUGUST

Is it the second or the third flush of roses? They are repeating just as they are supposed to. The lawn can look a little tired in drier periods now, while some of the earlier summer flowers are past their best and, if left alone, can take the edge off the border's appearance. Some early summer herbaceous flowers, however, and even pyrethrums, are now producing a useful second crop. A variety of seedheads can be left alone: the developing pods of lilies, for example, can be very pleasing in form and character, while poppy and allium seedheads almost rival the blossom for interest.

Shrubs planted in the spring have now taken hold and are growing strongly, hardly recognisable as the little twiggy pieces bought in pots. Hopefully they have not been planted too close to neighbouring plants – this mistake is made all to easily, as the new plant scarcely ever looks capable of reaching the size it boasts of on the label or in the catalogue.

The compost heap grows daily with grass cuttings, weeds and the waste growth of earlier flowering plants. Rotted compost can now be distributed to the deserving shrubs and other plants.

A day or two of rushed tidying is carried out before setting off for the summer holiday. It is nice to get away; is it better to get back? Then we will notice a sea change in the garden: there is already a token premature fall of leaf from trees and shrubs that are perhaps finding drought a little difficult to deal with; amongst the other plants there are the first opening heads of Michaelmas daisies and, if these are opening, then autumn cannot be far away. Bulbs have already begun to feature heavily in the garden centres – has another year really gone so quickly? The autumn sales are beginning; it must be close to summer's end.

tasks
FOR THE
month

CHECKLIST

- Carry out the final spraying of the year against pests and diseases
- Check the design of your garden and move evergreen shrubs as necessary
- Continue mulching
- Purchase bulbs for planting immediately
- Take cuttings of evergreen shrubs
- Arrange for the care of your houseplants while you are on holiday

DEADHEADING
This is done to encourage fresh flowering and to produce a tidy effect. A sharp pair of secateurs or flower cutters in one hand and a glass of sustaining liquid in the other is the chosen method of the easy gardener!

LESS USUAL BULBS

Allium, onion species
Camassia, all, especially
C. leichtlinii caerulea
Erythronium
Fritillaria species
***Ipheion uniflorum* 'Wisley Blue'**
Ornithogalum species
Sternbergia lutea
Trillium

SPRAYING

Before going on holiday it may be worthwhile walking round the garden to see if any plagues threaten. A quick spray with an insecticide may prevent a population explosion whilst you are away. Roses and other plants such as michaelmas daisies that might become disfigured with mildew and other fungus troubles can be protected by a dose of a systemic fungicide. You are unlikely to need to do any more spraying after this until next year.

MOVING SHRUBS

This is one of the good times – while everything is in full growth – to check the details of your overall garden design. There could well be shrubs that have outgrown their places and will need to be either moved or sacrificed.
  Evergreen shrubs that need to be moved can be lifted and repositioned this month if they are watered very thoroughly first and then moved with a considerable rootball of soil. After repositioning they will need watering in again. The trick is to move the shrubs before they have got too large and to complete the whole operation quickly.

- Dig a trench all round the shrub a little beyond its branch spread.

- Many evergreens are surface rooting, with relatively few anchoring roots going down deep. Excavate in from the trench and below the shrub, until you end up with it as a detached entity with a large mass of soil held together by the fibrous root system.

- It is relatively easy to move a smallish specimen by lifting it on to a strong plastic sheet and then pulling the whole thing to the new site.

- It will take longer to achieve this with larger specimens, but the principle remains the same. Feed strong plastic sheeting, perhaps reinforced with ropes, under the shrub's rootball. If one, or even two people, cannot pull this along, use a rope tied to a sit-on mower to haul the package gently into position.

MULCHING

There are many good times for mulching and this is certainly one of them. Lawn mowings can be scattered thinly around shrubs and herbaceous plants to save steps to the compost heap. Layers of humus of varying sorts spread over the soil surfaces will help improve soil structure, moisture retention and insulate the soil from excessive heat, cutting down on watering.

PURCHASING BULBS

The garden centres begin to display their new supplies of bulbs for autumn planting this month. They may well try new things but are cautious about purchasing too much stock that they might find more difficult to sell, so you need to be there to pick and choose from these less plentiful items — some suggestions are listed in the margin.

There is another reason to be hovering around as the new displays are made: some bulbs, although offered as prepacks with pretty pictures, do not enjoy being out of the ground too long, and trilliums and erythroniums, for example, are best bought and planted early in leafy soil.

TAKING CUTTINGS OF EVERGREEN SHRUBS

A large number of evergreen shrubs can be propagated easily by taking cuttings now and rooting these in a frame or even in the open out of the wind.

■ Cut pieces 10-15cm (4-6in) long.

■ Remove the bottom few leaves and insert the base in hormone rooting powder.

■ Push the cuttings to at least half their depth into a gritty soil or compost. Do not allow it to dry out.

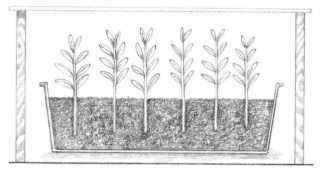

■ Cover with polythene or glass or place in a frame to prevent transpiration.

HOUSEPLANTS ON HOLIDAY

The easiest way to make sure your houseplants are looked after whilst you are away is to leave them in the care of a knowledgeable friend or relative. Alternatively, move the plants to a cool place, standing them on a good thickness of capillary matting that is itself standing on a waterproof base, perhaps polythene sheeting in a bath. The sheet should help minimise the danger of any discoloration of the bath or container.

A soaked piece of capillary matting will retain moisture in a cool, enclosed place for a considerable time. If the pots are watered before you leave they should last out for a normal break of ten days to a fortnight. For longer periods you may have to use a simple trickle irrigation unit if there is nobody to check the plants. If trickle irrigation is used, there should also be a drainage point, such as in a bath.

EVERGREEN SHRUBS FOR CUTTINGS

Brachyglottis (Senecio) 'Sunshine'
Cistus
Escallonia
Hebe
Olearia

plants
OF THE
month

WATER LILIES

New water lilies can be introduced into the pool from spring until the end of the summer, lowering them in special plastic net baskets filled with loam based compost or good garden soil from which any rotting leaves or weeds have been removed. Keep the soil in the basket in place by a generous layer of gravel. One tip — before lowering the planted basket, water it thoroughly to force out as much air as possible. Lower the baskets in stages if the plants are in leaf so that the pads float on the surface at all times as they grow, rather than being dragged deep below the surface.

NYMPHAEA 'PINK SENSATION'

type	Hardy perennial water plant with rhizomatous rootstock which looks like tubers
size	Spread 2-3m (6-10ft)
foliage	Tough, round, floating 'pads' 20-25cm (8-10in) across
flowers	Large, rich pink cups with a boss of golden stamens. Free flowering, mid- to late summer
site	Open, sunny water 30cm-1m (1-3ft) deep
care	Remove failing leaves
propagation	Divide in late spring or early summer every three or more years

NYMPHAEA 'ESCARBOUCLE' AND ODORATA

WATER PLANTS

PLANTS FOR A 23cm (9in) DEEP SHELF

Iris ensata, **Japanese flag**, purple, mauve, pinks or white, 60cm-1m (2-3ft), early-midsummer
I. laevigata, narrow foliage, blue flowers, 60cm-1m (2-3ft) early-midsummer
I. pseudacorus, **yellow flag**, robust native, 1.2-2m (4-6ft),early-midsummer
Mimulus ringens, **monkey musk**, lavender, 30cm-1m (1-3ft), summer and autumn
Myosotis scorpioides 'Mermaid', water forget-me-not, blue 15cm (6in) all summer
Pontederia cordata, **pickerel weed**, dark spear-shaped leaves, blue flowerheads, 50-75cm (20-30in), late summer
Sagittaria japonica, **arrowhead**, golden-centred white flowers, 45cm (18in), summer
Typha laxmannii (T.stenophylla), **reed mace, false bullrush**, 75cm-1m (30in-3ft)
T.minima **tiny reed mace**, 45-60cm (1½-2ft)

RODGERSIA AESCULIFOLIA

NYMPHAEA 'ESCARBOUCLE'

(and *N. odorata*)

type	Hardy perennial water plants with rhizomatous rootstocks
size	Spread 2-3m (6-10ft)
foliage	'Escarboucle' has dark green leaves, *odorata* apple green leaves
flowers	'Escarboucle' is considered one of the finest of water lilies, a rich crimson, glossy red. A connoisseur's flower, large and perfectly formed. *Odorata*, sometimes listed as 'Odorata Alba', has cup-shaped white flowers which are heavily scented
site	*Odorata* is best in water 30cm-1m (1-3ft) deep, 'Escarboucle' in water 1-1.2m (3-4ft) deep

NYMPHAEA 'MARLIACEA CARNEA'

type	Hardy perennial water plant with rhizomatous rootstock
size	Spread 2-3m (6-10ft)
foliage	Dark green, round leaves
flowers	Semi-double rose-pink blooms from mid- to late summer. One of a series of cultivars introduced over a hundred years ago and still well worth growing
site	Open, sunny water 60cm-1m (2-3ft) deep
care	Remove old leaves before they pollute the water
propagation	Divide in spring or early summer when the plant becomes crowded

RODGERSIA AESCULIFOLIA

All the rodgersias in commerce are splendid foliage plants. Whilst they can be grown in normal garden soils, there is no doubting their love of moisture – this is reflected in the size and height of the leaves. The flower plumes can be attractive too!

type	Hardy herbaceous perennial with creeping rhizomatous rootstock. For pond margin
size	Height 40cm-1m (16in-3ft), depending on soil and its moisture content
foliage	Large, shining, palmate leaves like those of a horse chestnut, with an impressed network of veins. Rich green, usually evenly suffused reddish bronze
flowers	Midsummer plumes of many tiny pinkish-red blossoms held well above the leaves
site	Excellent as a pond margin plant
soil	Moist
care	Strong-growing plant best out of strong wind
propagation	Spring divisions of the tough surface rhizomes will soon form their own clumps
other species	*R. pinnata*, 1-1.2m (3-4ft), pink flowers *R. podophylla*, 1.2m (4ft), cream flowers in rounded head *R. sambulifolia*, 1-1.2m (3-4ft) cream flowers in sprays

MARGINAL PLANTS

FOR WET SOIL

Astilbe, red, pink, white, 30cm-1m (1-3ft)
Dryopteris dilatata, broad buckler fern, 1m (3ft)
Gunnera manicata, huge leaves, only for large ponds, 2m (6ft)
Hosta in variety
Lysichiton americanus yellow skunk cabbage, early golden spathes, 75cm-1m (2½-3ft)
L. camtschatcensis, spring, white spathes, 75cm (2½ft)
Osmunda regalis, royal fern, 2m (6ft)
Primula, candelabra types, reds, oranges, yellows and white
Trollius various, globe flower, yellow and gold, 60cm (2ft)

WATER LILIES

'American Star', semi-double, deep pink
'Attraction', semi-double, deep red
'Gladstoniana', semi-double, white
'Gonnère', full double, white
'James Brydon', double, orange crimson
marliacea 'Chromatella', semi-double, yellow
odorata 'Sulphurea Grandiflora', semi-double, soft yellow

'Gladstoniana, 'James Brydon' and 'Chromatella'

practical project

MAKING A POND

Making a garden pool requires some effort, but a well-constructed pond will give a great deal of pleasure and require little upkeep.

CHOOSING SITE AND SIZE

An open site is needed, clear of trees and major shrubs so that rotting leaves in the water do not discolour it and produce toxic materials. The sun should shine on the water, and the pool should be easily seen from the main viewpoints such as the living room windows. Near the house a geometrical pool may look more in keeping; an informal one is easier to manage for wildlife.

A very small pond is difficult to look after. Water temperatures fluctuate dramatically and the balance of life is difficult to maintain. If possible, the very minimum water area should be 3sq m (3sq yd).

LINERS AND PREFORMS

Making a natural pool with a water-holding clay base is not a usual option. For small pools the normal choice is between preformed plastic/glass fibre and making use of flexible lining material. Ordinary polythene is not recommended; it is inflexible and easily punctured. Treble-laminated polythene is much better and can be purchased with a fifteen-year guarantee. However, altogether better is butyl rubber lining, a very tough, persistent material used for pools and lakes of considerable size. Initially more expensive, you pay very little, if any, extra if you calculate the cost over the many years of a butyl-lined pond's life.

EXCAVATION AND PROFILE

▪ Mark out the shape of the pool with a hose-pipe or length of rope. The margin of the pool should be level. Do not trust your eye – a spirit level is needed. 'Natural' pools should have gently curved margins, and will look less man-made if one end is wider than the other.

▪ For a prefabricated pool, excavate the soil and ensure that the bottom is as flat as possible so that the inserted pool is completely level. A layer of sand may make it easier to arrange this and ensure that the fit is tight.

▪ With liners, the pool can be 45cm (18in) at its deepest to allow for plants needing deep water. Around most of the margin a shelf about 23cm (9in) deep and 30cm (12in) broad is useful for the plants that would be drowned in the deeper part. Keep the sloping sides within a 20° angle.

CALCULATING LINER SIZES

▪ *The size of liner needed for your pond can be calculated as follows:*

The longer dimension = the pond length + twice the measurement of the sloping side + twice the margin flap of 25-30cm (10-12in).

The lesser dimension = the pond width at the widest part + twice the measurement of the sloping side + twice the margin flap of 25-30cm (10-12in) ▪

FILLING AND MARGINS

▪ Once the excavation has been completed, any awkward stones and sharp projections should be removed. The base and sides can then be made safe by either trowelling on a layer of damp sand or lining the entire hole with an old carpet.

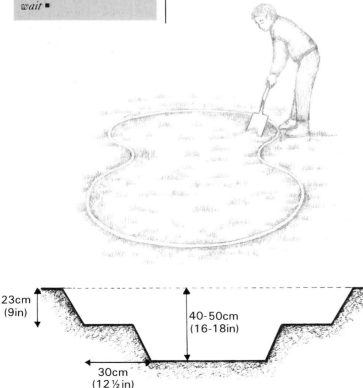

23cm (9in)

40-50cm (16-18in)

30cm (12½in)

■ Spread the liner over the hole and hold down the edges loosely with stones or baulks of timber. There should be enough liner to allow a flap around the margin of at least 30cm (12in).

■ Once the pool has been filled with water the edge of the liner can be trimmed to an even amount all round, perhaps 25cm (10in). Cover this flap with a layer of turf, rocks, stones or gravel. Stones overlapping the pool margin slightly will conceal any raw edges even before marginal plants begin to provide cover.

TIMESCALE

■ Time to make a pond will depend on its size and help available. It is best not rushed and could occupy two or three weekends ■

Wildlife will be encourged if a portion of the margin slopes gently into the water. Amphibians can get in and out easily and birds may reach the water. Suggested plants for the pool shelf and margins are listed with Plants of the Month p90.

OXYGENATING PLANTS

Elodea canadensis, Canadian pondweed
Hottonia palustris, water violet
Lagarosiphon major, common fish weed

POOL MAINTENANCE

Divide water lilies every third of fourth year in late spring. Cut off fully grown leaves. Cut off side 'branches' with plenty of healthy rootstock to make new plants. Discard the worn out centre.

Submerged oxygenating plants will need curbing regularly. Do not pull out lumps: use scissors and cut away and discard one-third of the plants.

The presence of green algae normally signals that the balance of plant and fish life is not right, and usually this means there are not enough plants. Algae with hanging filaments can be dredged out quite simply. Chemical treatment purchased from a garden centre can affect only a temporary cure and may be used as a new pool establishes itself and whilst a good balance of plant life is achieved. Introducing chemicals into established pools may damage wildlife.

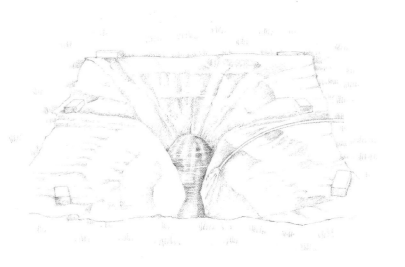

plants
OF THE
month

HYDRANGEAS

Of all summer-flowering plants, the hydrangeas must be top or very close to the top of the list for the easy gardener. They grow steadily in most soils, making impressive wide bushes either singly or planted severally in a sweep. They bloom freely and for great lengths of time. They need little attention. Finally, the dried flowerheads can be used for indoor flower arrangements through the winter.

HYDRANGEA 'TOKYO DELIGHT'

type	Hardy, deciduous shrub
size	Height 2m (6ft), spread 2.5m (8ft)
foliage	Clean, broad, pointed rich green leaves
flowers	Lace-cap type with wide flowerheads surrounded by impressive large, flat, sterile blooms in pale blue
site	Full sun or partial shade

HYDRANGEA 'TOKYO DELIGHT'

soil	Well drained with adequate moisture
propagation	Layer low branches in early summer
other cultivars	There is a large range of other *H. macrophylla* cultivars

HYDRANGEA PANICULATA
(Floribunda)

type	Hardy deciduous shrub
size	Height and spread 3m (10ft)
foliage	Well furnished with large, broad, pointed dark leaves
flowers	Towards late summer, each shoot ends with a large, tight, conical head of white flowers, the numerous small, central fertile ones encircled by large sterile ones in the manner of lace-caps. These flowers are white with a tiny red eye. Durable blossom
site	Open site in full sun or partial shade
soil	Reasonable with good drainage
care	One of the hardiest of all the genus. With reasonable soil and drainage, all it needs is the space to do its splendid duty. Hard spring pruning produces larger flower heads
propagation	Layer branches in early summer
other cultivars	'Brussels Lace', large pointed panicles of tiny fertile flowers ringed by larger white infertile ones

HYDRANGEA PETIOLARIS

type	Hardy, deciduous, self-clinging climber
size	Height 15m (50ft). Will reach up almost any wall
foliage	Broad, fresh green, typical hydrangea leaves
flowers	Lace-cap type. Once established, very free with wide heads of frothy little fertile flowers ringed by large, sterile ivory-white ones
site	Will grow up any wall or strong tree trunk. Useful for difficult cold or shady walls
care	Simple plant to grow. Will get away fast if newly planted specimens have their twigs tied into close contact with the wall.
propagation	By layering or air layering

HYDRANGEA PANICULATA 'FLORIBUNDA'

HYDRANGEA 'WHITE WAVE'

type	Hardy, deciduous shrub. Lace-cap type
size	Height 2.5m (8ft), spread 3m (10ft)
foliage	Healthy, broad, pointed leaves
flowers	Generous numbers of lace-cap flowerheads, small ivory fertile ones ringed by milk-white, wide, flat sterile ones. Very long lasting in bloom, midsummer to early autumn
site	Grows well in full sun but is at its best in half shade
soil	Like all the strong-growing hybrids, enjoys good, drained soil that does not dry out
propagation	Layer low branches early summer
other cultivars	'Pink Wave', similar but pale pink; 'Blue Wave', more correctly 'Mariesii Perfecta', an outstanding lace-cap with rich blue blooms very freely produced

practical project

GROWING FLOWERING CLIMBERS

Walls, fences and various other supports take on greater significance in the smaller garden. It is a waste of space to ignore the house walls where many flowering climbers can frolic to very good effect, often interweaving one with another, providing spectacular cascades of flower in return for relatively little work on the part of the gardener. We return to this theme on p132, but here we look at some of the flowering kinds that can make use of the space afforded by all sorts of supports, including other shrubs with more backbone and, of course, trees.

Always keep in mind the possibility of planting two climbers more or less together, a pair that work in tandem, with perhaps one blooming in spring and another later in the year. Clematis species and forms, for example, can link up effectively with roses, and the space has been used twice over.

The clematis and honeysuckle clans are the most important and glamorous of climbing genera, but there are many others. There can be few sights more overwhelming than an old, well-flowered wisteria, but roses, jasmines, passion flowers, solanums and climbing hydrangeas and their relatives all have their charms and useful attributes. These are the climbers proper; there are other shrubs that enjoy support and will go a long way upwards with this help even if they are not self-clinging and do not twine around supports – see the plant lists in the margin.

Cold and shady walls are the most difficult to clothe. Nevertheless, the lists show that there are many flowering climbers for these sites.

CLEMATIS SPECIES AND HYBRIDS

Clematis species need little pruning. *C. montana* clambers over anything handy, reaching 6m (20ft) in a very short time. In late spring it produces masses of four-petalled, square flowers in various pinks or creamy-white. Rather less extrovert is *C. macropetala* with nodding blue bell flowers. Later, from midsummer onwards, the very vigorous *C. tangutica* conjures up thousands of rich golden flowers followed by silky seedheads. Nicknamed the 'orange peel' clematis, the thick-petalled, rich-coloured *C. tibetana vernayi* blooms in summer and autumn. The only pruning needed with these is to halt takeover bids for space for which you have other plans. See p133 for further details on pruning clematis.

HONEYSUCKLES

Lonicera periclymenum is the honeysuckle that decorates our hedgerows. There is a later-flowering form 'Serotina' with richly coloured flowers of burgundy, cream and yellow that is magnificent from midsummer and well into autumn. This is a bigger genus than most gardeners realise, and contains many very attractive species and hybrids. One or two that ought to be tried are:

- *L.* × *brownii*, with brilliant orange-scarlet, crowded trumpet flowers.

- *L. etrusca*, from the Mediterranean, with highly perfumed flowers of yellow and orange-red that start opening in midsummer and continue perhaps until late autumn.

- *L. tragophylla*, with very large flowers of shining yellow in bunches of perhaps twenty at a time through the summer.

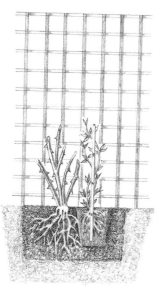

Passiflora caerulea

CLIMBERS AND SHRUBS FOR COLD AND SHADY WALLS

Camellia japonica **cultivars**, evergreen shrubs, red, pink or white flowers, early spring

Celastrus orbiculatus, twisting climber, male and female plants, tiny green summer flowers followed by autumn black fruits splitting to show yellow and red seeds

Chaenomeles **cultivars**, deciduous shrubs, red, orange, pink or white flowers, winter and early spring

Clematis × jackmanii **cultivars**, climbers flowering from midsummer onwards

Cotoneaster **species**, evergreen and deciduous, white or pink spring flowers, orange or red berries in autumn

Hydrangea petiolaris, self-clinging deciduous climber, cream flowers, summer

Jasminum officinale, scrambling climber needing support, white flowers, summer and autumn

Lonicera tragophylla, honeysuckle, twisting climber, yellow flowers, early summer

Pyracantha, evergreen shrubs, white flowers, yellow, orange or red coloured berries

Schizophragma integrifolium, self-clinging relative of hydrangea

CLIMBERS AND SHRUBS FOR WEST AND SOUTH WALLS

Abelia floribunda, slightly tender shrub, red summer flowers

Camellia sasanqua **cultivars**, evergreen winter/spring flowers

C. saluenensis, evergreen, early spring flowers

C. × williamsii **cultivars**, evergreen, winter/spring flowers

Ceanothus **species and hybrids**, evergreen shrubs, blue flowers, spring, summer and autumn

Chaenomeles **cultivars**, deciduous shrubs, red, orange, pink or white flowers, winter and early spring

Chimonanthus praecox, **wintersweet**, deciduous shrub, winter blossom, yellow and maroon

Clematis × jackmanii **cultivars**, climbers

Escallonia **cultivars**, evergreen shrubs, white, pink or red flowers, early and midsummer

Euonymus fortunei, 'Emerald n' Gold', evergreen with predominately golden foliage, inconspicuous flowers

Hedera, ivies, evergreen and very useful in variegated forms, flowers only on adult wood

Jasminum nudiflorum, **winter jasmine**, yellow flowers throughout winter

Lonicera **species and cultivars**, honeysuckles, various colours, summer and autumn

Osmanthus delavayi, evergreen shrub, fragrant white blossom, mid- and late spring

Parthenocissus quinquefolia, Virginia creeper, deciduous self-clinging climber, quickly covers a wall, shining green five-part leaves that turn brilliant colours in autumn

Passiflora caerulea, passion flower, climber, blue, purple, white, summer and autumn

Pileostegia virburnoides, self-clinging climber, white and cream, late summer and autumn

Rosa, climbing kinds

Solanum crispum, scrambling evergreen or semi-evergreen climber, purple and gold, summer

S. jasminoides, potato vine, scrambling climber, pale blue, autumn

Wisteria, twisting climbers, lilac or white, late spring, early summer

LARGE-FLOWERED CLEMATIS

There are very many fine kinds, including:

'Barbara Jackman', mauve-pink with dark stripes, summer

'Beauty of Worcester', dark violet double in summer and single in late summer

'Comtesse de Bouchaud', pale mauve-pink, summer

'Hagley Hybrid', deep pink, summer

'Marie Boisselot', white with cream anthers, summer

'Mrs Cholmondeley', rich lavender, early summer

'Nelly Moser', pink with maroon stripes, early summer

'The President', dark violet, early summer

ANNUAL CLIMBERS

These are easily grown and can be allowed to scramble over existing plants and supports to add a generous portion of colour and interest through the summer and autumn. Try:

Cobaea scandens, the cup-and-saucer flower, for a warm wall. Raise seedlings in heat

Humulus japonicus lutescens, golden-bronze, large palmate leaves

Ipomoea purpurea, morning glory, height 2-2.5m (6-8ft). Sky-blue trumpets from early summer to early autumn

Lathyrus odoratus, sweet pea

Tropaeolum majus, nasturtium. Climbing kinds can be very effective, especially on poor soil, early summer into autumn

T. peregrinum, canary creeper, height 2-2.5m (6-8ft). Deep-cut blue-green foliage and lots of frilled lemon flowers with long spurs, summer until frosts

SEPTEMBER

Here comes the autumn, and the season of mists and mellow fruitfulness. In the countryside trees and shrubs begin to turn colour, and in the garden this can be concentrated by the juxtaposition of the best autumn-colouring plants from all continents. We may have the maples from America and Britain's spindleberry (Euonymus europaeus), *the guelder rose* (Viburnum opulus) *and the wild cherry* (Prunus avium). *From Asia we have* Spiraea thunbergii *in brilliant red and vines like the huge-leaved* Vitis coignetiae, *and many berberises such as* B. wilsoniae *and* B.thunbergii *in vivid scarlets and reds.* Berries and other fruits are advertising their presence in the most extrovert of hues, and a blazing rather than mellow fruitfulness comes over dozens of shrubs led by contoneasters, pyracanthas and Malus *(crab apple) forms.*

There are no hard-and-fast lines drawn until the first real frosts of autumn, which usually start next month. Summer flowers linger, but more and more of the real flowers of autumn are appearing. Gardeners that tend such things have chrysanthemums and dahlias of all sizes. For the easy gardener the smaller, hardy chrysanthemums make more sense: the ones that do not have to be sprayed, or disbudded, or talked to every day. Among Michaelmas daisies, grow the ones that are resistant to mildew. Hugely floriferous rudbeckias in gold and orange will highlight the Michaelmas daises from the other side of the colour spectrum. And suddenly, where the soil was bare and leafless come the naked flowers of colchicums and crocuses, together with the wonderful Nerine bowdenii. *What a splendid dispensation that one species of the genus is hardy – and certainly if we were to pick one nerine to be hardy most would choose* N.bowdenii.

tasks
FOR THE
month

LAWN SEED MIXES

Numbers refer to parts

ORNAMENTAL QUALITY

8 Chewings fescue *(Festuca rubra commutata)*

2 browntop bent *(Agrostis tenuis)*

GENERAL USE WITH RYE GRASS

3 perennial rye *(Linum perenne)*
3 Chewings fescue
2 smooth-stalked meadow *(Poa pratensis)*
1 lesser Timothy *(Phleum bertolonii)*
1 browntop bent

GENERAL USE WITHOUT RYE GRASS

4 smooth-stalked meadow
3 Chewings fescue
2 creeping red fescue *(Festuca rubra rubra)*
1 browntop bent

SHADY AREAS

5 rough-stalked meadow *(Poa trivialis)*
3 wood meadow *(P. nemoralis)*
2 creeping red fescue

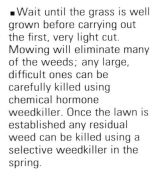

STARTING A NEW LAWN

Early autumn is a good time to make a lawn either by sowing seed or laying turf. Seed involves less physical effort and usually provides the better quality of lawn; turf is harder work to lay but produces a 'finished' lawn more quickly. Thorough preparation pays big dividends whichever method is chosen.

■ Kill off all permanent weeds using a glysophate weedkiller.

■ Lay field pipes if the site is poorly drained. Good drainage helps keep the surface healthy and makes it less attractive to moss.

■ Work over the soil well using spade and fork or a rotovator.

■ Ensure that the surface is level so that water does not gather in pools and all the grass receives equal water and nutrient supplies.

Sowing seed

Various mixtures of grass seed are on sale, and one of the main distinctions is between those containing rye grass and those without. If the lawn has to do duty as a playground for children a hardwearing grass mix with rye grass will be best. If you want a bowling-green lawn you need a mix excluding rye grass and with a high proportion of fine fescues and bent species. The list in the margin gives some examples.

■ Allow 80-100gm (3-4oz) per sq m/yd, which is quite generous. It may be easier to distribute the seed evenly using a seed-sowing machine, often loaned free from seed suppliers. However, it is not all that difficult to scatter the seed by hand, walking first length and then width-ways.

■ Rake lightly after sowing. Do not roll.

■ Wait until the grass is well grown before carrying out the first, very light cut. Mowing will eliminate many of the weeds; any large, difficult ones can be carefully killed using chemical hormone weedkiller. Once the lawn is established any residual weed can be killed using a selective weedkiller in the spring.

Laying turf

Success with turf depends on its quality and how well it is laid. Turf produced from seed ensures a quality product that is weed free. It is more expensive than meadow turf, although this can also be good, especially if the weeds have been killed.

■ Lay the turves on the well-prepared site, making sure that each is butted tight up to the next.

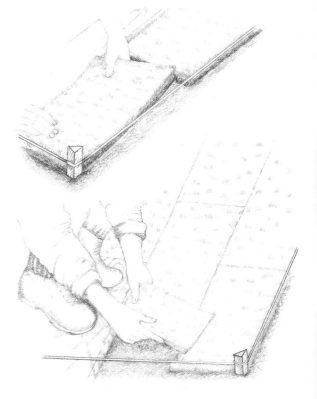

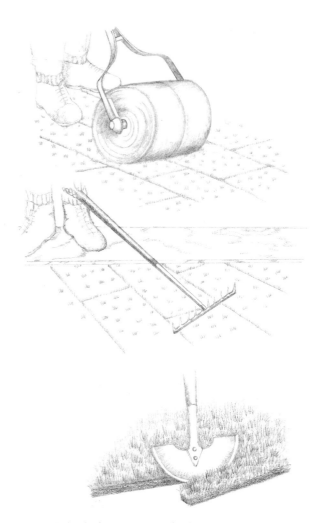

■ If possible lay before forecast rain, and certainly avoid doing anything in a mini-drought. See p41 for more details.

PLANTING BULBS

Early autumn is the ideal time to plant bulbs for spring bloom. The soil is likely to be moist and not too hard to pierce, and the bulbs will absorb the moisture and get quickly into root action, thereby ensuring the best rate of increase and flowering performance.

Check that the bulbs are planted at their correct depths (see p105). Bold groups of a limited number

of cultivars are usually much more effective than a confetti effect from many kinds.

TIDYING THE HERBACEOUS BORDER

This enterprise is a rather more active matter through the summer and into the autumn than in the spring if everything is tidied up for winter. In spring it will then be merely a matter of seeing off germinating weed seed and perhaps spot killing one or two troublesome perennial weeds.

A 8-10cm (3-4in) layer of shredded bark is a great timesaver as it will inhibit

most weed seed, and any that manages to germinate is pulled out very much more easily. It also provides an excellent soil-protecting mulch, and keeps everything looking tidy. In early autumn any spot, where for one reason or another the bark layer has been badly breached, can be filled up with a bucketful or two of fresh bark.

Tidying the herbaceous border now may well go hand in hand with propagating some of the herbaceous plants.

PROPAGATING HERBACEOUS PLANTS

The spring- and early-summer-flowering, clump-forming herbaceous plants may well be ready for propagating now, and this early start will ensure that the new pieces are well rooted and established before the winter.

Lift the clumps, force two forks through the centre back to back and then ease them apart to break up the clump. Discard the older rootstock from the centre and make fresh plantings from the much livelier growths around the edge. There is a temptation to propagate more than you need, especially of easily split plants. Be ruthless and put the surplus on the compost heap or through the shredder – unless you have family or friends who need plants.

In some cases, plants may be just nicely established by the early autumn and yet you are anxious for more. Pieces can then be detached from the edge without lifting the whole plant, using a strong craft or gardener's knife to sever a rooted piece. Then dig it up with a trowel and plant it in its new station.

HERBACEOUS PLANTS TO PROPAGATE BY DIVISION

Achillea, yarrow
Aconitum, monks hood
Astrantia, masterwort
Aster, early-flowering kinds
Bergenia
Chrysanthemum maximum, shasta daisy
Dicentra, bleeding heart
Doronicum, leopard's bane
Erigeron, fleabane
Epimedium
Geum, avens
Hemerocallis, day lily
Lamium, deadnettle
Ligularia
Monarda, bergamot
Physostegia, obedience plant
Polygonatum, Solomon's seal
Primula
Pulmonaria, soldiers and sailors
Rodgersia
Tiarella, foam flower
Trollius, globe flower

plants
OF THE
month

**TROUBLE-FREE ASTER
AMELLUS CULTIVARS**

Recommended for open spots
where their easy nature makes
them useful autumn flowers, these
Michaelmas daisy cultivars are
attractive to butterflies and neat
mannered towards the front of the
bed or border:

'Brilliant', upright, deep pink,
50cm (20in)
'King George', violet and yellow,
50cm (20in)
'Moerheim Gem', violet and
yellow, 40cm (16in)
'Nocturne', large, lilac-blue, erect,
60cm (2ft)
'Pink Zenith', clear pink, 35cm
(14in)
'Sternkugel', large, lavender blue,
50cm (20in)
'Violet Queen', see main text

ASTER AMELLUS 'VIOLET QUEEN'

Aster amellus forms are dwarf and sturdy. They
can be planted and left for several seasons if
you wish. However, they will perform better if
lifted regularly in early spring and split up;
they do not like to be split in autumn. They
are completely resistant to mildew and so are
definitely easy garden plants.

type	Hardy, herbaceous, clump forming perennial
size	Height and spread 30-40cm (12-16in)
foliage	Dark green, spear-shaped leaves
flowers	Very rich violet, semi-double flowers with a central orange-gold disc. Durable heads of blossom in early to mid-autumn. A very fine cultivar
site	Sun or semi-shade
soil	Well-cultivated soil that does not dry out
care	Mildew-resistant, neat grower
propagation	Split clumps in early spring, not autumn
other cultivars	See margin

ASTER × FRIKARTII

Even those prejudiced against Michaelmas
daisies will look on this cultivar with favour. It
blooms over such a long period and is so
disease resistant and trouble free that it
deserves a place in most gardens.

type	Hardy, herbaceous perennial. One of the best for mixed borders

size	Height 80cm (32in), spread 60cm (2ft)
foliage	Dark green, pointed, rough
flowers	Rich lavender-blue daisies with smallish central discs of limy-yellow turning more honey-coloured with age. Widely branched with flowers over many weeks from midsummer until late autumn
site	Airy, open site in bed or border; full sun or semi-shade
soil	Well worked
care	Bushy, open growth with widely branched flower stems means that it may need some support if there are no surrounding plants to help hold stems more or less upright. Resistant to mildew
propagation	Best divided in early spring
other cultivars	*A.f.* 'Mönch', *A.f.* 'Wunder von Stäfa'

BLUE WOOD ASTER
(Aster cordifolius)

type	Hardy, herbaceous perennial
size	Height and spread 1m (3ft), but in the wild there are varied populations with some plants only 10-12cm (4-5in) tall. In cultivation some variants in good soil can reach 1.5m (5ft)
foliage	Low leaves are spear-shaped, with heart-shaped bases near the stems, and are rough to the touch. Dark dull green. Stem leaves are narrowly heart-shaped

ASTER AMELLUS 'VIOLET QUEEN'

ASTER NOVI-BELGII 'FREDA BALLARD'

flowers	Much-branched, arching stems carry hundreds or even thousands of small daisies (1.25-2cm (½-¾in) across) with relatively wide petals. The colour can be a good blue for an aster, but most of those grown in the garden are near white, a very pale lilac or pink flushed. The palish yellow centres become darker honey and pinky-purple with age
site	Happy in full sun or in quite a deeply shaded spot
soil	Well worked
care	Unless grown amongst low shrubby support this species is best staked or grown through pea sticks. Good resistance to mildew
propagation	Easily increased by early spring division
other cultivars	*A.c.* 'Silver Spray', height 1.2m, spread 1m (3ft), white blush pink

ASTER NOVI-BELGII 'FREDA BALLARD'

Picking just one from the *Aster novi-belgii* Michaelmas daisies is almost impossible, especially as they seem to look best in association with others of their type. A collection of half a dozen can bring the garden alive in autumn, when many look a little tired. These types can get mildew, but by replanting annually and spraying with systemic fungicide the plants can be kept pristine.

type	Hardy, herbaceous perennial. One of the hybrid race most gardeners identify as true Michaelmas daisies
size	Height 80cm-1m (32in-3ft)
foliage	Dark green, pointed leaves
flowers	Many quite large, doubled flowers of rich purple-toned red. This free-flowering hybrid opens before many of its type in early autumn but lasts for many weeks
site	Best in an open, partially sunny spot
soil	Well-worked with adequate moisture through the summer
care	New hybrids like this one are somewhat better able to cope with mildew, but plants are best sprayed regularly, perhaps every three weeks. If you cannot bother with this confine your choice to cultivars of *Aster amellus*, *A. novae-angliae* and some of the species. These seem to be either resistant or nearly so
propagation	Best repropagated each spring – by tearing off a few fresh rooted pieces or taking cuttings
other cultivars	'Marie Ballard', blue; 'Blondie', white with cream buds; 'Patricia Ballard', pink; 'Sandford's White Swan', white. Dwarfs 'Alice Haslam', red; 'Peter Harrison', rose pink; 'Professor Anton Kippenberg', blue; 'Snowsprite', white

ASTER SPECIES

Apart from the standard Michaelmas daisies, there are a number of interesting and attractive, easy character species. Here is a short selection:

A. thomsonii 'Nanus'
Compact form 45cm (18in) tall, early flowering, large saucer-shaped blooms, narrow mauve-blue petals, small yellow centres

A. sedifolius
Narrow leaves, 60cm (2ft) stems with myriads of rich mauve stars. Early

A. ericoides
Very thin leaves and lots and lots of tiny flowers, almost a misty cloud in mid- to late autumn, 1m (3ft). White and lavender forms

A. laevis 'Callioppe'
A form that can reach 2m (6ft). Dark green leaves and almost black stems. Many lilac flowers in the second half of autumn

A. thomsonii 'Nanus'

A. ericoides 'White Heather'

practical project

NATURALISING BULBS

The idea here is to plant bulbs so that they look as if they are growing naturally and, once planted, can be left to spread and flower each year, producing sheets of colour in exchange for very little work indeed. Some genera are ready to fall in with this plan, and within these are some species and cultivars that are more successful than others.

Snowdrops and winter aconites are a must because they bloom so early and will persist and increase with almost no further attention. You can hasten their increase by lifting clumps some weeks after flowering, splitting them and replanting immediately (see p41).

Daffodils can be found still flourishing that were planted a century ago. Nowadays the most successful are the somewhat smaller kinds, such as the very good early-flowering *Narcissus cyclamineus* hybrids (see p43). These are half or two-thirds the size of the normal, larger garden kinds and so are daintier, have less foliage and are not so liable to wind damage. Almost as important as anything, they seem more in scale with today's modest sized gardens.

SIX SIMPLE STEPS TO SUCCESS

■ The bulbs will be going into permanent quarters, so pick suitable long-term sites: for instance, rough grass, not the lawn. Bulbs can also look especially good between shrubs and in the equivalent of light woodland. Make sure that they will not be quickly grown over by heavy shrubs, especially evergreens.

■ Ensure that the bulbs are planted deeply enough. Shallow bulbs increase quickly by splitting into many small pieces which are too small to bloom. It is better to plant a little too deep than too shallow: see the planting depth guide.

■ Try to plant in natural rather than geometrical shapes, and certainly not in square blocks.

■ Do not plant mixtures. Each group should be of one kind so that the flowers come out together to make the greatest impact.

■ Allow leaves to die down naturally if possible. If you need to tidy over planted areas, wait several weeks after blooming before cutting the leaves (daffodils require six weeks).

■ If you want to feed naturalised bulbs this can be done in the very early spring by giving the planted areas a dusting of potash (sulphate of potash or dry collected wood/bonfire ash). Alternatively, the leaves can be sprayed with a foliar feed.

PLANTING BULBS

Using a sharp spade, cut three sides of a square in the turf or soil, lift, plant, and replace.

Eranthis hyemalis

Narcissus cyclamineus

Anemone nemorosa

Lilium martagon

Allium cernuum

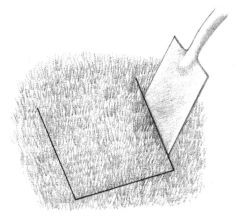

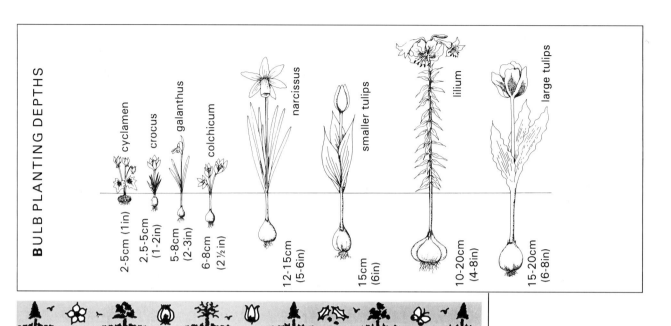

BULB PLANTING DEPTHS

cyclamen — 2-5cm (1in)

crocus — 2.5-5cm (1-2in)

galanthus — 5-8cm (2-3in)

colchicum — 6-8cm (2½in)

narcissus — 12-15cm (5-6in)

smaller tulips — 15cm (6in)

lilium — 10-20cm (4-8in)

large tulips — 15-20cm (6-8in)

GOOD BULBS FOR NATURALISING

plant	height	description	flower
Allium aflatunense 'Purple Sensation'	*80–100cm (30–36in)*	large, round violet heads on strong stems	late spring early summer
A. karataviense	*15–20cm (8–12in)*	huge flowerheads 15cm (6in) across, white shaded steely violet. Fine seedheads, leaves, 12cm (5in) wide	late spring
Allium moly (golden garlic)	*20–30cm (8–12in)*	clusters of golden flowers	summer
Anemone blanda	*10cm (4in)*	blue, white or pink flowers (see p27)	spring
Anemone nemorosa (wild anemone)	*10cm (4in)*	white flushed pink, rarely blue (see p27)	spring
Colchicum	*15cm (6in)*	white, mauve or pink (see p114)	autumn
Crocus tommasinianus	*5–8cm (2–3in)*	many narrow silvery mauve buds, opening to stars (see p27)	early spring
Cyclamen hederifolium	*5–8cm (2–3in)*	lots of pink or white flowers. Attractive marbled foliage (see p115)	autumn
Eranthis (winter aconite)	*8–10cm (3–4in)*	golden buttercup flowers (see p26)	winter
Galanthus (snowdrop)	*10–15cm (4–6in)*	white (see p22)	winter
Lilium martagon	*1–2m (3–6ft)*	nodding, curled up mauve pink flowers, sometimes white, 6–50 per stem	early summer

Narcissus cyclamineus hybrids (see p42)

BULBS FOR LONG-TERM, TROUBLE-FREE EFFECT

Anemone nemorosa, wind flower
Eranthis hyemalis, winter aconite
Galanthus, snowdrops
Lilium martagon
Narcissus 'February Gold'
N. 'Jenny'
N. 'Jumblie'

WARNING

■ *Most bulb-planting gadgets are expensive failures. They are difficult or impossible to press into any but the softest stone-free soil, and a spade or fork is usually a much more reliable and efficient tool* ■

plants
OF THE
month

FLOWERING
CLIMBERS

CLEMATIS MONTANA RUBENS

The glamorous, large-flowered hybrid clematis take everyone's eye, but there are many species that provide important garden plants. None is easier or more useful than *Clematis montana* in all its forms, included here as an important flowering climber, though it flowers in late spring.

type	Hardy, deciduous climber with tendrils
size	Height 3-10m+ (10-30ft+)
foliage	Tripartite, pointed-lobed leaves, grey-green
flowers	Four-petalled pink, 4-5cm (1½-2in) across, boss of pale yellow anthers, late spring. Prolific bloomer on the previous years' wood
site	Strong grower which will cover walls, sheds and screens, or grow over stumps and up trees
soil	Most garden soils
care	Needs little attention. Prefers its roots in shade. After flowering, if necessary cut away broken stems and growth that is trespassing beyond its bounds. Most plants can be left to get on with life without any attention

propagation	By layering or 10-15cm (4-6in) softwood cuttings in early summer
other cultivars	The *C. montana* type, creamy white; 'Elizabeth', a little larger and soft pink; 'Tetrarose', much bigger in leaf and flower, leaflets 8-9cm (3-3½in) long, flowers up to 8cm (3in) across

HONEYSUCKLE 'LATE DUTCH'
(*Lonicera periclymenum* 'Serotina')

Most garden centres carry a considerable choice of clematis, but honeysuckles are less in evidence, although there is a range of different species and hybrids, mostly climbers but also some free-standing shrubs. Not all the vividly coloured climbers are scented, but in the one profiled here you have everything. It is a wonderful selection from the species that decorates the hedgerows.

type	Hardy, deciduous climber with twisting stems
size	Height 6m+ (20ft+)
foliage	Mid-green leaves, greyish underneath, oval or almost oblong in form
flowers	Very generous, crowded heads of rich burgundy, pink and creamy-

LONICERA PERICLYMENUM 'SEROTINA'

PRUNING CLEMATIS
The species need no real pruning, just tidying of dead wood and some discipline when they have strayed too far. For C. montana and other early kinds this will be done after flowering.
The early large-flowered cultivars blooming on last year's wood from early to late summer are pruned before growth starts, but this consists only of removing dead wood and cutting back shoots to strong buds showing in the leaf axils, these buds producing the first crop of bloom.
The later-flowering kinds of the jackmanii type are pruned before growth begins – at the end of winter or in early spring. Prune away all top growth down to two strong buds at the base. Provide support for the growth which will produce the flowers in summer and autumn.

(See also practical project (pp132-3)

white becoming yellow. Flowers long-tubed and heavily perfumed, mid- to late summer and well into autumn

site Grows easily in sun or shade

soil May be somewhat more floriferous on poorer soils

care Very easy, quick grower which needs little attention. Does not need feeding. An eye should be kept open for aphids, which can be sprayed if they threaten to become a nuisance

WISTERIA SINENSIS

Can any climber be more lovely than a well-established wisteria growing with good support, so that the long bunches of flowers hang down to best advantage? The genus is found in Japan, China and North America, and happily all are very hardy and especially good growing on support against sunny walls. The species profiled here is from China, and was introduced to the rest of the world in 1816.

type Hardy, deciduous, long-lived shrub, climbing by twining stems

size Height 10m (30ft)

foliage 30cm (12in) long pinnate leaves of 11-19 ovate leaflets. Mid-green. Foliage begins to expand when the plant is already in full bloom. Leaves are dropped over a long period in autumn

flowers 20-30cm (8-12in) drooping, grape-like racemes of lilac pea flowers. Mid-late spring. Often a small flurry of bloom in the autumn

site Sunny spot

soil Well drained

care Grows strongly in good, well-worked soils. Once the framework of branches is established, to induce generous flowering the plants need pruning strongly, cutting back laterals close to the main branches twice a year, once after flowering and again in late summer

varieties *W.s.* 'Alba', white; 'Black Dragon', slightly smaller racemes in dark purple; 'Prematura' and 'Prematura Alba', same as the types but bloom freely as young plants; 'Prolific', a particularly vigorous cultivar which produces longer lilac racemes to perhaps 35cm (14in)

SOLANUM CRISPUM 'GLASNEVIN'

SOLANUM CRISPUM 'GLASNEVIN'

The most popular solanum must be *S. tuberosum*, the potato, but it is a large genus of more than a thousand species including herbs, shrubs, trees and, here, a very robust and valuable climber.

type Evergreen or nearly evergreen scrambling, open climber, hardy in warmer areas and possible in other parts in warm wall sites

size Height 3.5-10m (12-30ft)

foliage Dark green, pointed oval leaves up to 10cm (4in) long

flowers Particularly free, early and midsummer, bunches at shoot ends. Potato flowers in purple, with golden anthers pointing from centres

site South and west walls suit it best

soil Any reasonable drained soil

care Grows rapidly but needs some support

propagation By softwood cuttings in early summer

HONEYSUCKLES TO TRY

Lonicera caprifolium, yellow, white and pink, scented

L. etrusca, creamy-yellow suffused red, becoming richer yellow later. Scented

L.e. 'Superba', larger bunches of flower

L. × italica, yellow and burgundy

L. tragophylla, largest flowers, shining yellow, unscented

practical project

CREATING EASY BORDERS

BEDDING PLANTS
To save work resist the lure of bedding plants which can take a lot of time and effort. If you have unexpected gaps in your beds/ borders a dash to the garden centre for a few stand-ins is permissible.

Iris sibirica

Beds and borders are the main decorative parts of most gardens. So that they have some shape all round the year, it is sensible to have some permanent features guarding against winter bleakness and giving a design backbone throughout the year. Both evergreen and deciduous plants can provide shelter and a backcloth for the lively herbaceous actors. You may find that in time your shrubs take over the whole and then there will be even less need of maintenance. Some useful shrubs are listed in the margin.

HERBACEOUS PLANTS

Some herbaceous plants take more looking after than others. Tall kinds may need supporting; others grow so rampantly they need lifting and dividing each year and only a small piece is retained. There are others that once planted will provide annual performance with little attention for decades. Usually the best effect is obtained by planting a limited number of bold groups rather than trying to accommodate one of everything that takes your fancy.

TROUBLE FREE PERENNIALS

The table below lists some of the many perennials that can be used in beds and borders and will not require a lot of attention once planted. The removal of dead foliage at the end of winter is almost the only chore.
* = evergreen or semi-evergreen.

plant	height x spread	description	flowering period
Acanthus mollis			
	1.2m (4ft) x 60cm (2ft)	magnificent foliage; white and purple flowers	summer
WHITE MUGWORT			
Artemisia lactiflora	1.2-1.5m (4-5ft) x 50cm (20in)	plumes of cream and white	summer
Aruncus dioicus (A. *sylvester*, Goat's beard)			
	2m (6ft) x 1.2m (4ft)	creamy plumes; dark foliage	midsummer
SIBERIAN BUGLOSS			
Brunnera macrophylla	45cm (18in) x 60cm (2ft)	sprays of blue forget-me-not flowers; good for dry spots	early spring
Clematis integrifolia			
	75cm (30in) x 75cm (30in)	mauve-blue bells	summer
BLEEDING HEART			
Dicentra spectabilis	75cm (30in) x 50cm (20in)	hanging pink-red and white flowers	spring
CONE FLOWER			
Echinacea purpurea	1.1.2m (3-4ft) x 50cm (20in)	rosy-purple wide-petalled daisies, with raised central cone	summer

plant	height x spread	description	flowering period
Geranium spp. and cvs. – many			
	variable	blues, purples, pinks, whites	spring and summer
*Helleborus argutifolius			
	40-50cm (16-20in) x 1m (3ft)	pale green flowers	midwinter to spring
*H. orientalis hybrids			
	40-45cm (16-18in) x 40-45cm (16-18in)	white, cream, yellow, mauve, purple, near black	late winter and spring
HOSTA – many			
	variable	mainly white and lilac, attractive foliage	summer
Inula ensifolia 'Compacta'			
	23cm (9in) x 23cm (9in)	many golden daisies	early summer to early autumn
SIBERIAN FLAG			
Iris sibirica	50cm-1m (20in-3ft) x 75cm-1m (2½-3ft)	blue, dark-veined; narrow foliage; moist soil	late spring to early summer
Paeonia hybrids – many including 'Bowl of Beauty'			
	1m (3ft) x 1m (3ft)	rosy-pink flowers with white and golden centre	spring and early summer
SOLOMON'S SEAL			
Polygonatum multiflorum	75cm-1m (2½-3ft) x 75cm-1m (2½-3ft)	white bells, marked with creamy-green, arching stems	early summer
LUNGWORT – many			
Pulmonaria spp. and cvs.	20-30cm (8-12in) x 40-80cm (16-32in)	blue, pink, white; some with spotted foliage	spring and early summer
FOAMFLOWER			
Tiarella cordifolia	15-23cm (6-9in) x 30-45cm (12-18in)	white, frothy spikes; leaves sometimes bronze-flushed	spring and early summer

Other useful plants include – *Macleaya cordata* (p82), *Nerine bowdenii* (p115) and *Rodgersia aesculifolia* (p91)

SHRUBS

EVERGREEN

Berberis darwinii
B. × stenophylla
Camellia × williamsii 'Donation'
Cistus, rock roses
Eleagnus pungens 'Maculata'
Erica, heathers
Genista, brooms, evergreen effect
Mahonia japonica
M. × media 'Charity' and other hybrids
Olearia × haastii
Pieris formosa forrestii
Rhododendron
Skimmia japonica
S. reevesiana
Viburnum davidii
V.tinus

DECIDUOUS

Abelia
Acer japonicum, maples
Aralia elata 'Variegata'
Berberis thunbergii cultivars
Chaenomeles, flowering quince
Cornus alba 'Sibirica', dogwood
Cotinus coggygria, smoke bush
Hamamelis, witch hazels
Hydrangea
Philadelphus, mock orange cultivars
Rosa species and bushy hybrids
Spiraea 'Arguta'
S. × vanhouttei
Viburnum bodnantense 'Dawn'

EASY-BORDER MAINTENANCE

■ **Suppress weeds by planting ground cover**

■ **Inhibit weed germination and impressive soil structure by mulching with shredded bark or well-rotted humus compost**

■ **Kill perennial weeds by spot spraying with a systemic weed-killer**

■ **Prune ugly branches from shrubs**

■ **Check and control the spread of strong herbaceous plants**

OCTOBER

There is no doubt about it. The autumn is here. The first real frosts arrive this month. There are leaves everywhere. We begin to look kindly at the evergreens that seem to have better manners, but on a crisp morning there is some pleasure in gathering the fallen harvest and piling the leaves on to the compost heap.

This is the month to look to the colour of the countryside and those gardens and arboreta that take on a festive air for a few weeks. In our own gardens we can marvel at the colour of individual trees and bushes, and some that can be overlooked at other times are extraordinary now in their autumn dress. The coloured fruits of crab apple species and hybrids, pyracanthas, thorns and berberis are richly painted, and there are the unusual ones like the vivid violet bunches of Callicarpa bodinieri giraldii 'Profusion'. Birds may welcome the chance to feed on some berries, but they seem to regard most of the shining harvest as a supplementary store to leave for later.

We are surrounded by the daisy-flowered compositae in full cry, chrysanthemums, Michaelmas daisies and asters of all sorts. Colour is heaped on colour as the lowering sun lights up the scene. It is the end of the growing year, but in the end there is a beginning and new flowers are appearing. Autumn crocuses arrive suddenly, the few of last month quickly becoming a multitude. Colchicums continue to open, all sparkling fresh and naked of leaves. Viburnum farreri *has been opening flowers before the month began but now, having dropped its foliage, it shows off its wares to better effect, as do the hybrid kinds led by the ubiquitous and wholly admirable* V. bodnantense 'Dawn'. Mahonia japonica *has flower sprays developing and the rounded buds on the witch hazels betoken midwinter blossom.*

tasks
FOR THE
month

CHECKLIST

- [ ] Bring tender plants under cover
- [ ] Plant out spring favourites
- [ ] Collect and store seed
- [ ] Gather material for compost making
- [ ] Tidy up diseased plant material and prune shrubs and fruit trees
- [ ] Plant up containers and bowls of bulbs
- [ ] Give the lawn its final cut and rake over to remove moss
- [ ] Check tree stakes

PLANT SAVING

This month it is high time to bring into a frost-free, airy shelter those plants that would otherwise perish: the fuchsias, geraniums (pelargoniums), begonias, gladioli and dahlias.

Cut back fuchsias quite severely, and strip off a lot of the lush leaves and detritus from geraniums. Leave begonias to die down gently, still with a ball of soil around their roots, but squash geraniums and fuchsias into the smallest pots that will take their roots and keep them almost, but not absolutely, dry until they are ready to be started into growth again in the spring.

Dahlias and gladioli should be lifted, shaken free of most soil, and placed in a frost-proof, airy spot to dry out further. Begonias, dahlias and gladioli can be given a final clean when fully dry. Store gladioli in paper bags or, better still, plastic net bags, perhaps hanging from a shelf in the garage. Treat dahlias and begonias with a fungicide dusting or spray before storing in a dry and frost-free place.

In mild winters and areas free from heavy frosts, dahlias and gladioli can survive without lifting, but often they will then come into growth rather late and may not do as well as expected. *Gladiolus nanus* and similar small-flowered varieties grown near a warm wall can do very nicely for several years without lifting.

PLANTING

Where there are obvious gaps from clearing summer plants that are not to be filled by bulbs, take the opportunity to push in a few wallflowers, sweet williams, forget-me-nots and polyanthus. This is not to suggest a bedding scheme, but the late spring would be all the poorer without the scent and sight of these stalwarts, particularly wallflowers. These have long been offered as bundles of seedlings pulled out of the soil almost without working roots, but nowadays it is often possible to find plants in plastic modules that are fully rooted and will establish themselves very much quicker and better.

SAVING YOUR OWN SEED

Some leading new plant cultivars have been bred by amateurs with little space, so why not save seed from some of your favourite kinds and see what happens? Earlier in the year you could have taken a hand in creating something new by transferring pollen from one cultivar to another.

Collect seed when ripe, just before it is likely to be split by the plant. Dry it by hanging seedheads upside

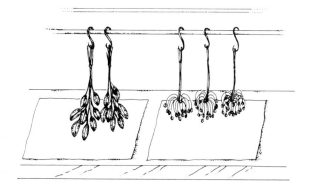

down over sheets of clean paper in a cool, dry, airy place, and store in labelled packets in dry, cool conditions until it is time for sowing, or sow immediately. Sowing as soon as the seed is ripe is often sensible, and certainly means the job is not overlooked in spring.

MAKING COMPOST

At this time of year there is plenty of material for composting: fallen leaves, late grass cuttings, torn up bedding plants, prunings and waste litter. The more diverse and thoroughly mixed this is, the more likely it is to rot down quickly and thoroughly. It may well be worth gathering material for a week or two, then mixing it thoroughly and placing it on the current heap.

TIDYING THE GARDEN

The easy gardener need not worry too much about tidying the garden for winter. Do not be in a hurry to cut down the clumps of dead foliage of ornamental grasses, but take time to enjoy the colour and form of the clumps, their fawns and beiges lit by winter sunshine. Leave the seedheads of sedums, Michaelmas daisies and many others to provide subdued colour and form, and for the birds to peck amongst them, seeking seed and insects to keep fragile bodies fed.

Nevertheless, there is still some tidying to be done. Any diseased plant tissue not previously dealt with should be disposed of now, while pruning of fruit and ornamental trees and shrubs to encourage next year's growth is a matter of tidying, of hygiene and of maximising next season's crops.

PLANTING UP CONTAINERS

Summer containers can now be emptied. Rather than leave them redundant, fill them up again with winter-flowering pansies, bulbs and perhaps even heathers and ivies.

Pots and bowls of bulbs for indoor flowering should be organised now if they have not already been seen to. Make it a rule to leave all potted bulbs in a cool spot for a minimum of eight weeks, before bringing them into the mild warmth of a cool greenhouse or conservatory to start into quicker growth. The eight-week period will ensure that the bulbs have all made extensive root systems that can then benefit from the extra warmth and consequent acceleration in growth metabolism. They will then be ready to take a final jump into the living room as they come into bud.

Plant hyacinths singly in separate pots and, when on the point of opening their first 'pips' of flowers, arrange several of equal status in a bowl and pretend that all has been done in one fell swoop.

LAWN CARE

Grass growth is much slower now but you will need to go over proper lawns two or three times more – do not set the blades too low. Rake over any mossy areas thoroughly, first one way and then at right angles, to try to loosen as much of the moss as possible. You can spike the lawn now if you are a fanatic; it could help surface drainage.

CHECKING TREE STAKES

Before the more boisterous of the gales get under way, it is prudent to check any stakes used to support relatively newly planted shrubs or trees. They may have worked loose or even rotted. Make sure that everything is firm, and remember that trees are best secured only 30cm (1ft) or so from the soil. The aim is to keep the *rootstock* still; the trunk should manage for itself and its cell structure will build up strength to withstand the gales that are inevitably going to come its way.

plants
OF THE
month

COLCHICUM 'LILAC WONDER'

The colchicums are splendid large flowers to
give a bright, fresh look to corners of the
garden in autumn, when some plants are looking tired. Remember that the leaves that come
in spring are very large, so plant where these
will not cause annoyance.

type	Large corm
size	Height at flowering 15–20cm (6–8in)
foliage	Large, shining, rich green, erect oval leaves 20cm (8in) long appearing in spring
flowers	Large goblets of glowing pink with a pale throat, appearing in mid-autumn. Possibly the best of the hybrids
planting	Plant with 7–10cm (3–4in) of soil over the corms
site	The leaves can be a little excessive and are best between shrubs that may help to screen them partially as they begin to die down
soil	Open, well drained
propagation	Divide corms as soon as the leaves die down. Increases very well
other varieties	See margin

COLCHICUM 'LILAC WONDER'

CROCUS SPECIOSUS

Of all the autumn-flowering crocus species
this is quite clearly the garden leader, blooming freely and increasing well. The flowers are
showier than most, but once you have a patch
of this nicely settled in you could add some of
the other species to give an extended season
and variety.

type	Hardy corm
size	Height at flowering 10cm (4in)
foliage	Typical narrow leaves with a central white rib appear at the end of winter

flowers	Many leafless, large globes of violet-blue with darker veining and brilliant orange stigmata. Early and mid-autumn
site	Sunny. Between shrubs, in the border, rock garden and light grass
soil	Well drained
care	This is the best and easiest of the autumn-flowering species
propagation	Increases well. Divide corms after leaves have died down in late spring
varieties	*C. s. albus*, excellent white; 'Cassiope', large rich violet; 'Oxonian', darkest violet-blue, orange stigmata. See margin for other recommended species

CYCLAMEN HEDERIFOLIUM

There are several very fine hardy cyclamen species. This one is the best for foliage, flower form and colour, hardiness and all-round good temper.

type	Hardy, very long-lived tuber in the form of a round disc
size	Height at flowering 8–10cm (3–4in)
foliage	Attractive and variable, usually ivy shaped with silvery patterning around a dark centre. Worth growing for the leaves alone
flowers	Perfectly formed cyclamen flowers in glowing pinks, darker at the centre. Usually starts blooming in early or mid-autumn and carries on for several weeks. First blooms usually appear before the leaves.
planting	Do not buy old collected tubers. Plant young potted seedlings that will do much better, they are often in bloom and can be planted then
site	Plant in sun or semi-shade where the tubers can be left undisturbed. Very adaptable between shrubs, at the base of trees, in the border, hedgerow or rock garden
soil	Drained soil with humus
care	Plants can last for many decades and, although they can be moved, are best left undisturbed
propagation	Flowering plants will provide large seedpods which ripen in late spring. Fresh seed germinates easily in open ground or in pots
other varieties	White forms look lovely and make an excellent contrast between the pinks. See margin

NERINE BOWDENII

NERINE BOWDENII

Nerines come from South Africa, so enjoy warm conditions and dislike wetness. Happily, the one hardy species is also one of the best.

type	Large, hardy bulb, the only hardy one of the genus
size	Height at flowering 45–60cm (18in–2ft)
foliage	Glossy, strap-like, arching leaves appearing in spring and usually dying down by midsummer
flowers	Up to ten vividly pink flowers to a head, with narrow waved petals in an open trumpet form, and protruding anthers and stigma
planting	Plant in early autumn or spring with the tip of the bulb only just below the surface of the soil.
site	Full sun. The base of a wall is ideal as the bulb needs summer baking
soil	Very well drained
care	Do not disturb until very crowded. Sometimes may stay over a decade without being lifted
other cultivars	Named cultivars are tender and should not be planted outside

RECOMMENDED HARDY CYCLAMEN

C. cilicium, small, pale pink flowers with a darker mouth. Leaves heart-shaped, usually with a silvery glaze. Autumn

C. coum, rounded dark leaves, squat purple-red, pink or white flowers from early winter through spring

C. hederifolium, see profile

Cyclamen hederifolium

practical project

MAKING A HEATHER GARDEN

LIME-TOLERANT HEATHERS

Erica carnea, winter flowering. Red, pink and white cultivars (see p22)

E. arborea, late winter, early spring. White, scented. Height 5m (16ft)!

E.a. alpina, hardier, half the height

E. × darleyensis, winter flowering (see p22)

E. erigena (E. mediterranea) Spring. Purple-red, pink or white. Height 60cm–1m (2–3ft)

E. vagans, Cornish heath, tolerates some lime. Midsummer to late autumn. Pink, mauve or white bells. Height 75cm (30in)

ACID-LOVING HEATHERS

Calluna vulgaris, wild heather. Many flower and foliage colours. Late summer and autumn flowering, dead flowerheads are attractive shades of rusty brown. Red, pink, mauve and white

Daboecia cantabrica, St Dabeoc's heath. Through summer and autumn, purple, purple-pink or white. Much branched, height 60cm–1m (2–3ft)

Erica ciliaris, Dorset heath. Dark green or greyish foliage. Summer, pink or white. Sprawling, height 30cm (12in) but wider

(continued opposite)

THE ULTIMATE IN EASY GARDENING

The heather garden may seem 'old hat', but it can score very highly for ease of culture, year-round effect and colour, and interest. It can be a very inexpensive piece of gardening and is not difficult to construct.

This is perhaps the ultimate in labour-saving, easy gardening. It makes equal sense in a small patch or in the wide acres of a stately home. Soil types need not matter: there is a good selection of heathers that thrive with lime; many more flourish in acid conditions. Heathers are also drought resistant, so summer hosepipe bans and watering worries can be thankfully forgotten.

SITE

Heathers from the wide-open spaces need an open site in the garden, and will not thrive in dense shade. Drainage should be good enough to prevent persistent sodden conditions.

Established heathers form a thick ground cover difficult for weeds to penetrate. Before planting, however, kill off all perennial weeds, including couch grass, docks, bindweed, ground elder, nettles and dog's mercury. Use a systemic weed killer and wait for a few weeks to make sure that you have made a good job of the spraying. If you missed a section, respray and wait again before starting to shape the ground into interesting contours and plant.

Whatever the scale, normally the best effect will be achieved if the beds have curved outlines. However, where this is impossible in a small garden, heathers can be colourful and very successful in a formal bed, perhaps even with a brick-built wall around the edge.

Some variation in the ground levels makes the whole arrangement much more interesting and natural in appearance. Gentle undulations can be exaggerated by planting the squatter kinds of heathers in the lower parts and taller ones on higher ground. It is extraordinary the difference a few inches can make.

USING A RANGE OF PLANTS

To avoid any feeling of sameness, a few dwarf conifers will provide a contrasting feature, their upright stance emphasising the character of the heathers. A few clumps of small bulbs can add exciting colours, the yellow of dwarf daffodils such as *Narcissus* 'Tête à Tête' making the pinks and purple-reds of winter heathers all the more telling. Even occasional herbaceous plants such as hellebores can be useful. But do not overdo these invited guests: remember it is the heathers' party.

PLANTING PLANS

When drawing up planting plans there are two things to remember. First, avoid a spotty effect. It is better to plant three or more heathers of a kind together to achieve a bold effect. Second, avoid regularity. Plant cultivars in natural shapes, not square blocks, and vary the size of the shapes. Try to arrange a contrast of colours and shades between different cultivars, bearing in mind not only the flower colour, but also their blooming period and, most importantly, the foliage colour. White forms are particularly useful for highlighting other colours.

Position any dwarf conifers so that they too look naturally placed – not one just plonked in the geometrical centre. Three in an irregular triangle, with the smallest somewhat closer to the edge of the bed, is sensible.

MAINTENANCE

Heathers, originally planted perhaps five to the square metre (square yard), will need weeding for a season or two until they meet and look after themselves. After that, a light

new level

original level

dwarfer kinds planted low, taller planted higher, to exaggerate the new contours

trimming with shears following flowering will be all that is necessary – and that only as plants get much older, and not always then.

PROPAGATION

Heathers are easily propagated by layering or from cuttings.

■ If compost is heaped around a branch in early spring, rooted pieces will be ready by autumn. These can be planted out or grown on in pots over winter.

■ Alternatively, lift a complete plant and plant it more deeply so that the lower half is under compost or sieved soil. If this is done in spring, there will be lots of rooted bits by autumn.

■ Cuttings 4–5cm (1½–2in) long can be taken late spring and early summer. Except for callunas, the lower leaves can then be stripped off, the bottoms dipped in hormone rooting powder, and the cuttings inserted in an equal mix of peat and rough sand. Keep them moist in a propagator or a pot or tray sealed in a clear plastic bag.

■ In warmth, rooting will have started in a fortnight. Start to open the cuttings up to the air, but still keep them carefully watered and shaded. Rooting takes longer in cool conditions.

■ After about two months the cuttings can be potted up and grown on in 8cm (3in) pots until they are ready to plant out.

TIMESCALE

■ *If you are making a heather garden or bed where there has been grass, you will need to allow several weeks to ensure that the weed-killer has done its job thoroughly. Digging or rotovating (much quicker) will follow, and then the ground will be raked into contours – this latter stage, plus planning, should take no more than a few hours for all but the biggest heather gardens* ■

Erica cinerea, bell heather. Summer and autumn. Clusters of bells in dark purple to magenta, pink and white. Tight shrub, height 15–30cm (6–12in)
E. tetralix, cross-leaved heath. Early summer until mid-autumn; red, pink or white. Open, spreading, height 20–30cm (8–12in)

DWARF CONIFERS TO GROW WITH HEATHERS

Juniperus communis compressa, upright pillar, height 30cm (12in) after 10 years, 38cm (15in) after 15 years
Thuya occidentalis 'Rheingold', slow-growing rounded pyramid, height 3–4m (10–12ft) after 20 years
Picea glauca 'Albertiana Conica', neat cone, height 2–4m (6–12ft) after 20 years
Pinus mugo 'Gnom', dwarf character plant, height 2m (6ft) after 10–20 years
P.m. 'Mops', dwarfer character plant, height 1m (3ft), spread 2m (6ft) after 10 years

SMALL BULBS TO PLANT IN GROUPS AMONG HEATHERS

Galanthus, snowdrops
Crocus species, especially:
   C. speciosus, violet, autumn
   C. tommasinianus, pale lilac, late winter to early spring
   C. biflorus and *C. chrysanthus*, white, yellow, orange and blue, late winter and early spring
Dwarf narcissi, **especially:**
   N. obvallaris, the Tenby daffodil, yellow; *N.* 'Jenny', white, early and mid-spring; *N.* 'Tête à Tête' and 'Jumblie', early, golden; *N.* 'Hawera', many headed, lemon, late;
Tulipa species, **including:**
   T. tarda, white and gold, mid- to late spring; *T. praestans*, many headed, orange, early and mid-spring; *T. turkestanica*, many headed, small, green/white and yellow stars, very early
Fritillaria meleagris, snakeshead fritillary, late spring into early summer
Muscari azureum, neat, early, sky blue, early spring

NOVEMBER

Now we can see the bones of the garden design – most of the leaves
that have to fall have fallen. The wisteria drops a quota each day,
a weary, somnambulant stripper. We give thanks for the
quickness of the Virginia creepers – once started, they have
everything on the ground in a week and we can tidy up.
At the beginning of the month we could be busy planting the last of
the spring bulbs; traditionally this is the tulip-planting month.
Shrubs and trees bought bare-rooted can be installed, firmly
supported to make light of gales to come.
Pruning implements come into play as the surgeon-gardener makes
decisions. Is this feathered, newly planted Prunus subhirtella
'Autumnalis' to grow as a low-branched specimen, or do we strip
off the lower branches to encourage a respectable trunk? Shall we
cut the roses back carefully, or heed the surprising research that
shows that bush roses bloom and grow as well, or better, when
topped with shears or a chainsaw to knee-height?
Rockery beds are not without interest. There can be late small bulbs
offering colour, and in peaty spots some brilliant blue gentians will
still be defying the weather. Make sure that they are not covered by
sodden fallen tree leaves, and a handful of gravel or grit spread
here and there will protect precious rock plants from wet around
the collar. Cold they can usually take, cold with wet can be fatal.
In the past, prunings and even autumn leaves would have gone on
the bonfire. Now much of the prunings go through the shredder to
make mulching or composting materials. A small residue of
diseased material still has to be burnt, but the bonfire ash can be
stored dry or scattered over the border. This potash is almost
worth its weight in gold; being so soluble it is best used when
growth is lively, so storing is worthwhile.

tasks

FOR THE

month

TIDY UP – NOW
Garden furniture that you meant to store away last month can be put away now after making sure that everything is dry and clean.

A TASK FOR BAD WEATHER
Greenhouses and conservatories used for plant growing can be cleaned and tidied during less clement weather when it is not possible to work outside. Fertilisers, composts and sprays can be replenished as needed. Trays and pots can be checked, cleaned and tidily stored.

LEAF MOULD
Collect all fallen leaves and make a contained pile which can be left to rot down for up to a year and will make a very useful ingredient for composts or mulches. Exceptionally good leaves to use are those of beech and oak.

CHECKLIST

- Plant trees and shrubs
- Prepare the garden for winter
- Dig over new beds and repair worn parts of the lawn
- Finish planting spring-flowering bulbs
- Clean and put away tools and machinery

PLANTING TREES AND SHRUBS

This could be the month for major plantings if you have decided on new shrubs and trees for your garden. With the prevalence and convenience of container-grown plants we have become conditioned into planting at all times of the year, which is convenient, but getting back to the old-fashioned idea of planting trees and shrubs in the autumn makes sense – early autumn if possible, but the first half of this month if not. At this time of year the plants, whether container grown or bare rooted, stand a chance of getting acclimatised and their roots into some sort of relationship with the new soil before the end of the winter and the beginning of really hectic growth activity as the soil warms in spring.

- Make a 'five-pound' hole for a 'one-pound' plant:

- Cultivate the soil well, removing the first spade's depth for at least 1m (3ft) for even a modest-sized shrub.

- Dig over the bottom spit. You can incorporate well-rotted material from the compost heap, mixing this with the soil that is returned once the shrub or tree is in position (see p36).

- It is not normally necessary to douse the soil with fertiliser at this time.

PREPARING FOR WINTER

Plants that are slightly tender and can be damaged by the excessive cold and wet of an exceptional winter, can be given some simple protection merely by adding an extra thickness of shredded bark mulch around their bases. If the rootstock can be saved from damage, even if above ground some injury is sustained, the plant will usually survive and grow away successfully next year. A generous covering of fallen autumn leaves is another useful, cheap and effective way of insulating the base of plants.

Encouraging birds
Birds are our unpaid, hardworking partners in keeping down garden pests – perhaps they should be paid by growing shrubs, trees and herbaceous plants that provide them with food and shelter. During the winter natural food can be augmented at a variety of feeding stations, on the ground and at various heights and places in the garden. The most successful sites will be those where the birds can approach from and retreat to tree and shrub cover. Birds will find slugs, snails and a multitude of

small insects that we can well do without. As relatively harmless insect life can often be encouraged by a loose scattering of rotting leaves and such debris through the winter, it is foolish to clear our beds and borders and leave them just as bare soil.

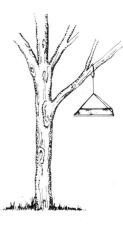

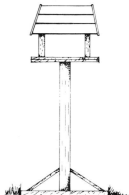

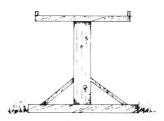

Deterring slugs and snails

There are places where it pays to be extra tidy or at least vigilant. Loose paving and other stones may provide shelter for slugs, snails and wood lice in remarkable numbers. You can either make sure that paving and stones are more securely bedded into their positions, or check periodically beneath and remove unwanted livestock. Pots, plastic trays, pieces of plastic sheeting, wood, glassware and other materials, often with smooth surfaces, can also be home to slugs and snails, so do not leave such things around the garden. It is a good policy at all times to leave out a number of slug traps (see p33) which are examined daily if possible, and slugs and snails collected.

Mulching

Check mulches of gravel around alpines, and of bark around shrubs and other plants and make good any thin patches. Mulches help provide good surface drainage and prevent soil freezing – the cause of evergreen plants suffering in winter.

Clearing paths

Sweep paths clear of leaves and other matter that can make them wet and dangerously slippery. If there are parts that are likely to be almost permanently wet, drainage should be provided to make sure that these areas can dry out and to discourage the formation of ice in cold snaps.

Trimming lawn edges

Trim lawn edges for winter to make them look neat and remove the clippings, together with any leaves in the gutter. Try to keep these edges snail and slug free, as they are likely to be close to the smaller border plants that can do without slug-led depredations.

DIGGING AND LAWN CARE

Keep off the soil when it is very wet – consolidating it by trampling all over will tend to ruin the soil structure. In open weather, any ground that is to be prepared for new beds can be deeply but roughly dug, leaving it lumpy for the frost to break down – let nature do the work for you.

Patches of lawn that have become worn can be repaired by taking out the affected part and replacing it with good turf. An alternative to transplant surgery is to dig over the area lightly, rake it down level to create seedbed conditions and sprinkle grass seed over it. Ideally, this would be done in early to mid-autumn or in early spring, but can be carried out as late as early this month.

PLANTING BULBS

You may have forgotten a clutch of spring-flowering bulbs you meant to plant some weeks ago – do not despair. Most bulbs will manage well enough if planted now, and certainly such things as tulips will be fine. Try to find a warm, very well-drained spot for tulips that you are thinking of leaving down for several seasons.

PUTTING THE MOWER TO REST

Your tools and machinery deserve good treatment. They have probably worked hard over the year. The mower should be cleaned thoroughly, the blades sharpened and its moving parts treated to a light coating of thin oil. You may think a professional overhaul worthwhile and a saving on your time and effort, but be careful – prices can sometimes be high and the work poorly carried out.

To repair broken lawn edges: cut out the broken piece, including some turf around it. Lift the turf with a spade so that it has a flat bottom. Turn it until the level edge is on the outside and the damaged area is contained within the lawn. Firm it in place then fill the hole with compost – adding some grass seeds to the top 1cm (½in). Water well.

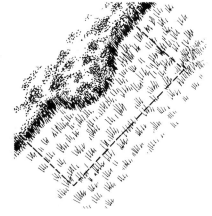

plants
OF THE
month

VIBURNUMS TO TRY

Other viburnums well worth considering include:

V. × burkwoodii, evergreen hybrid from **V. utile** and **V. carlesii**. In spring produces wide bunches of fragrant pink-budded, white blossom

V. carlesii, deciduous, dense, rounded shrub. Red-budded bunches of fragrant flowers open pinky, becoming white in spring

V. opulus, guelder rose, deciduous, good foliage that turns colour in autumn. Lace-cap flowers in late spring, followed by impressive bunches of glistening red fruits

V. plicatum 'Mariesii', deciduous, horizontal branches balancing lots of wide, flat heads of lace-cap flowers in late spring

VIBURNUMS

There are few genera more useful to the gardener than the viburnums. They are undemanding, healthy plants, usually with highly perfumed blossom. Apart from those featured below, there are a series of spring-flowering kinds such as Viburnum carlesii, which has lovely wide bunches of shining white flowers with the most appealing of perfumes. There are also several very good hybrids.

The native guelder rose, V. opulus, is one of the most magnificent of shrubs in autumn with huge, drooping bunches of vivid, polished red fruits and wonderful autumn foliage colours. V.o. 'Xanthocarpum' is a variant that weighs down its branches with huge crops of shining golden fruits. There is also a form with sterile flowers, therefore fruitless but with conspicuous large, snowball heads of ivory-white blossom.

Although not closely related to the hydrangeas, there is a species V. plicatum with lace-cap flowers and several forms, such as 'Lanarth', 'Mariesii' and V. tomentosum. These have a horizontally structured branching system with flat flowerheads with bunches of small, fertile flowers surrounded by large, sterile ones.

VIBURNUM DAVIDII

VIBURNUM RHYTIDOPHYLLUM

type	Hardy, evergreen shrub
size	Height and spread 4m (13ft)
foliage	Handsome cover of tough, dark green, oval, somewhat hanging leaves with impressed veins
flowers and fruit	Small creamy flowers crowded into a shallow dome of blossom 10–20cm (4–8in) across in late spring. Some seasons a lot of seed is set, the berries first a decorative red and then turning black
site	Useful at the back of the border or as part of a screen
care	Robust, long-lived shrub in normal soils
propagation	Layer low branches, using pieces about 25cm (10in) long

VIBURNUM DAVIDII

type	Hardy, evergreen, low shrub. Good foliage plant
size	Height 1m (3ft), spread 1.5–2m (5–6ft)
foliage	Impressive thick coat of rich, dark green leaves 8–12cm (3–5in) with very definite, unusual lengthwise main veins
flowers and fruit	Rather ordinary small white flowers in flat heads with pinky stems in early summer. If plants of

both sexes are present, the females will produce long-lasting bunches of very pleasing dark purple-blue fruits in autumn

site Sunny spot

soil Well drained

care Easy. As this is a species with both female and male forms, to get crops of the very handsome blue fruits you will have to plant both sexes in close proximity, perhaps one male to every four females

VIBURNUM × BODNANTENSE 'DAWN'

type Hardy, deciduous hybrid shrub. One of the *Viburnum × bodnantense* series bred from *V. farreri × V. grandiflorum*

size Height 3m (10ft), spread 2.8m (8ft)

foliage More or less oval leaves, with impressed veins and bronzed

flowers Very prolific, with tight posies of deep-pink-budded flowers that open paler pink or blush-white from late autumn through the winter. Fragrant. One of the finest winter-blooming shrubs

site Sunny spot

care Strong grower in normal soils

propagation Low twigs can be rooted easily by layering in the autumn and potted up as independent plants in a year's time

other varieties There are other named clones of the same breeding. 'Deben' has more gaunt, erect growth with very white blossom; 'Charles Lamont' is a generous bloomer, rather paler in effect than 'Dawn'

LAURUSTINUS
(Viburnum tinus)

type Hardy, evergreen shrub

size Height and spread 3m (10ft)

foliage Thickly furnished with smooth, oval, dark green leaves

flowers Large numbers of flat heads of pretty, small white flowers from the beginning of winter through into spring, but most prolific in the second half of winter. Pink in bud, scented

site Best in sun, but will tolerate some shade. Can be planted almost anywhere and is often used as a hedge or screening plant

care Trouble-free shrub. A great favourite in Victorian times and still worth growing

propagation Low pieces can be layered and rooted quickly – it will probably layer itself without any help – and rooted pieces can be moved to their new quarters in early spring

cultivars There are a number of named forms. 'Gwenllian' and 'Eve Price' are the present leaders

VIBURNUM 'DAWN'

practical project

DESIGNING FOR WINTER

TREES AND SHRUBS WITH INTERESTING BARKS AND FORMS

Acer griseum, paper-bark maple, flaking orange-brown bark. Also other maples

Betula pendula, silver birch

B. utilis var. jacquemontii, vividly white bark

Cornus alba, red stems

C.a. 'Spaethii', beautiful variegated foliage, red stems

C. stolonifera 'Flaviramea', olive-yellow stems

Eucalyptus niphophila, snow gum, jigsaw-patterned bark, green, grey, olive, silver, etc. Also other eucalypts

Rubus biflorus, whitewashed winter stems

R. thibetanus, upright and arching stems, painted white

Salix alba 'Britzensis', willow, pollarded for orange stems

S. daphnoides, purple stems often with plum-coloured 'bloom'

WINTER CHALLENGE

Officially it is still autumn, but the clothes are the clothes of winter and the garden is well into the coldest season. It is cowardly not to recognise the fact that this can be – or at least feel like – the longest season of all, and to plan for this time of year in the garden. In other parts of the book the importance of walls and the infrastructure, such as paths and screens, has been emphasised. Here we look at the *living* heart of the matter: what plants should you grow to make your surroundings colourful and interesting through these months? And how should you deploy them?

In the easy garden trees and shrubs must play a leading role in the plan, with a lively balance between evergreen and deciduous types. The deciduous ones can contribute substantially with form, line and attractive bark colour and formation, while the evergreens provide mass and a range of foliage hues. The lists in the margin give plenty of ideas.

IN THE BACKGROUND

The far reaches of the garden are not visited and examined so closely in winter, and here you can have shrubs and trees forming screens but also acting as a backcloth against which others can act out their parts. Hollies may be dark rich green with or without berries, they may be lit up with cream or golden variegation. The pointed cone of the conifer, *Chamaecyparis lawsoniana* 'Lane' shines yellow and cheerful. Yellow and gold are very valuable to lighten up the darker greens, see list of such kinds from which to make a choice (right margin).

STATIONING FLOWERING PLANTS

Larger things may be planted further back, the winter flowering cherry, *Prunus subhirtella* 'Autumnalis', will signal its cheerful message from near or far, cheerful so long as we do not mistake it for a flurry of snow.

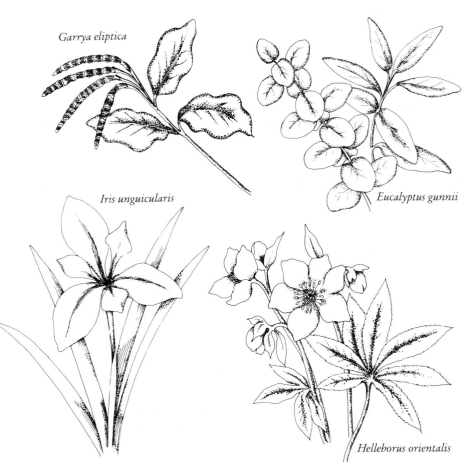

Garrya eliptica

Iris unguicularis

Eucalyptus gunnii

Helleborus orientalis

IN THE FOREGROUND

On the whole we ought to have winter-flowering plants close to where we can enjoy them without having to venture far into the hinterland. *Iris unguicularis* is nearby, it needs the warmth of a wall to persuade it that it is as happy as it would be in its native Algeria. Every form of this is worth having, the flowers are remarkably large and opulent for winter.

Winter flowers are often scaled-down versions of summer favourites. Like some of the winter honeysuckles, for example. *Lonicera fragrantissima*, *L. standishii* and their hybrid *L. × purpusii* have creamy flowers obviously moulded to honeysuckle design but smallish. They are still welcome, especially as they come in large numbers and are well perfumed.

PERFUME

Perfume is a recurring theme with winter flowers. Wintersweet, *Chimonanthus praecox*, is intoxicating. Just as well to have it close at hand growing up the house wall to give it the warmth it needs to bloom freely and to be appreciated. The evergreen mahonias, resplendent in armoured foliage, are bright with many terminal sprays of lemon-coloured, lemon-scented blossom. They provide foliage to enhance their flower.

CONTRASTS

The perfumed witch hazels are bare of any suggestion of a leaf, wide-angled branches are enwreathed with yellow ribbon flowers. Plant these against a dark background to set off the blossom. A yew hedge would be splendidly upmarket, a holly bush will serve as well or try rhododendrons. The dark matt green of *Garrya elliptica* shows off its tassel catkins and is effective underplanted with clumps of hellebores, Christmas roses, *H. niger*. The Lenten roses, *H. orientalis*, often flower before their time with mauve, purple, white, cream and yellow blossom variously spotted and decorated. We take heads off our favourites and float them in a wide bowl of water to enjoy them inside.

TREES AND SHRUBS WITH YELLOW AND GOLD EVERGREEN FOLIAGE

Chamaecyparis lawsoniana, Lawson's cypress, several good golden forms including 'Lane'
C. pisifera 'Filifera Aurea', spreading whip-like branches, bright yellow
Eleagnus pungens 'Maculata'
Euonymus fortunei radicans and cultivars
Hedera, ivy, various including 'Buttercup'
Ilex aquifolium holly, including:
  'Golden King', bold golden margins, female
  'Golden Queen', margined gold, male
  'Golden Van Tol', bright irregular gold variegation, many berries
  'Mme Briot', large leaved with bright golden margins
Also other hollies
Ligustrum ovalifolium 'Aureum', golden privet
Pinus sylvestris 'Gold Coin', striking golden pine
Taxus baccata 'Aurea', golden yew
Thuja occidentalis 'Rheingold', golden-yellow becoming bronze in winter
T. plicata 'Collyer's Gold', dwarf, light green and yellow
Also many other *Thuja* forms

BERRIED TREASURE IN WINTER

Cotoneaster, various, including
C. × watereri
Crataegus, various, including
C. × lavallei 'Carrierei'
Ilex, hollies
Malus, various, including **'Golden Hornet'** and **'Red Sentinel'**
Rosa various, including
R. moyesii and **R. rugosa** cultivars
Symphoricarpus racemosus, snowberry

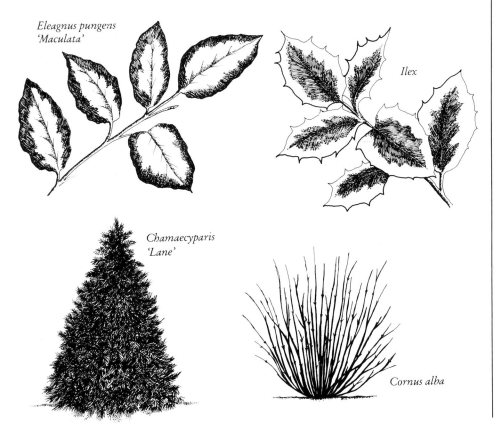

Eleagnus pungens 'Maculata'

Ilex

Chamaecyparis 'Lane'

Cornus alba

DECEMBER

This may be a cold, wet month, but the garden is still there and changing all the time. Clumps of daffodils are marking their place by pushing their first sheathed noses to the surface. There is life down there. Winter flowers are now on their own, not fraternising with the last lingering guests from the autumn party. Winter jasmine continues on its heroic way, fresh buds opening to replace heavily frosted ones. Viburnum tinus *does its splendid best as well as it did in a million Victorian gardens – old friends can be the best.* Viburnum × bodnantense *clones provide a thousand perfumed posies; the witch hazels and garryas are starting their frost-proof displays; bark and berry can be enjoyed. It is not a bad time.*

With winter weather outside, it is time to take a walk around the garden to pick as many different flowers to bring inside as possible. There are flowering quinces on the wall, a selection of heathers in full, belled bloom, the odd early spray of wintersweet, a camellia bud that is just opening, a clutch of hellebores as Christmas and Lenten roses and green-flowered species, the winter-flowering honeysuckles, small but scented and worth a close look, Iris unguicularis, *viburnums, primroses, a winter aconite, branches of winter-flowering cherry, and odd things that shouldn't be there like a calendula, a pink and an out-of-season gentian. Pansies, violas and periwinkles we expect to find winking open their winter eyes, but here and there wallflowers are showing colour months before they will be in proper bloom. And how curious that so many of these winter flowers have such generous scents – something we realise more fully when we bring them inside into the warmth.*

It is a time to give thanks.

tasks
FOR THE
month

CHECKLIST

- Dig up and discard unwanted plants
- Prune fruit trees and bushes
- Review your ground-cover plants
- Set up wildlife rest areas
- Check gutters and drains

make the most of every square inch.

PRUNING

Fruit trees and bushes can be left to their own devices and look highly decorative, but they are more productive if kept in some sort of order. This means pruning away weak, diseased and crowded wood to encourage healthy growth and the formation of plenty of fruiting buds (see p20).

Pruning should be completed before any spraying programme is undertaken. The easy gardener may decide that it is simpler and more economic to purchase fruit from the greengrocer than to try to grow your own. If so, it is pointless spending money on sprays to kill insects, clean the bark of moss and algae,

DISCARDING SURPLUS PLANTS

Most gardeners have quite a limited area in which to create their garden, and there is no point in continuing to grow plants that are time-consuming to look after and are not pulling their weight. A diseased or worn-out shrub can be a constant reproach – do something about it. You can make better use of the space, even if it is only to dig over, enrich the soil and replant with a decent specimen of the same plant.

It is as easy to grow the best form of a species or genus as it is one of the also-rans. In fact, new improved kinds can have bettter constitutions and hence be easier to grow, as well as having better flowers and overall appearance. There are plenty of good old kinds, but do keep an open mind and look at the newer things. You might as well

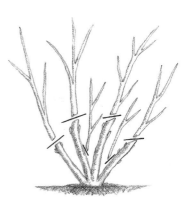
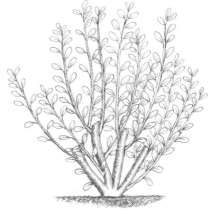
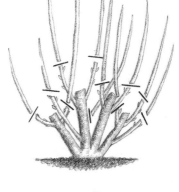

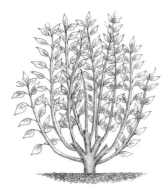
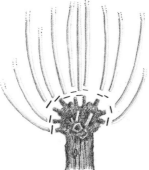

and to protect against fungus diseases. See the margin if you want to spray

REVIEWING GROUND-COVER PLANTS

Some ground-cover plants cover more ground than others, and there are some extremely vigorous ones that it may be prudent to look at and deal with now whilst they are relatively inactive.

Deadnettle, *Lamium maculatum* forms, for example, can romp away through the growing months and still make some headway at other times. It is more or less evergreen and excellent in many difficult areas, but a single piece will soon be 1m (3ft) across, so some curbing of its zeal may be necessary to prevent it swamping more choice and important plants.

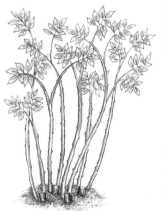

There may be some other ground-cover plants that you will wish to encourage. *Epimedium* species, tiarellas and hostas, for example, could be given extra room. The time to split these and expand their territory is the early spring.

More shrubby ground-coverers may need a little tidying. Pruning of odd branches that are poking in the wrong direction and removal of some awkward or damaged pieces may be necessary. The low growing cotoneasters such as *C. dammeri* and hybrids 'Gnom' and 'Skogholm' are normally very compact, tidy plants but may eventually grow wider than you require and need a little curtailing. Ground-cover roses are often perfectly all right with no attention but they can be cut back with shears or electric trimmer to keep them extra low and to encourage plenty of new growth next year.

Ivies, so useful covering ground in dark places where little else will grow, are energetic growers and will escape into more precious ground nearby if given half a chance. They can be simply trimmed back. Their foliage cover is dense and can be kept particularly neat and fresh by trimming the leaves off with a skimmer in late winter or spring. Obviously the colour variegated forms are more attractive than the standard dark green, even if the variegation does not show up so much in these dark places as it would in the sun.

WILDLIFE REST AREAS

It can be easiest to work with nature and we might as well encourage the wildlife that helps us to keep down pests and enjoy their company. This means being constructively untidy. For the obsessively tidy-minded, winter is an opportunity to get every last leaf picked up and making the garden look ready for a regimental inspection. If you feel the need to resist the temptation of making winter work for yourself why not allow certain areas for various 'wild' friends? Choose out of the way spots and leave them undisturbed. This is a good compromise and can be done without affecting the overall appearance of the garden.

Hedge bottoms provide shelter for field mice, hedgehogs and insects; a pile of wood logs does not need to be very massive to make an even more attractive home for these creatures. A few drain pipes or a pile of rocks left from year to year may become home to frogs, toads or slow worms. Behind the compost heap or hidden by shrubs leave loose leaves, grasses and grass clippings, straw and twigs. These areas will become tenanted by insects and so provide food for foraging birds as well as maybe housing the odd field mouse or shrew.

Leave the area behind the garden shed, summer-house or other building. It is not really looked upon as part of the garden scheme and is probably well away from the living house and so provides less temptation for tidying.

GUTTERS AND DRAINS

Before the wet winter weather really sets in a last check over gutters and drains is sensible. Climbers can quickly cause gutters to be blocked and the last of the autumn leaves can choke drains and pipes. Choose a fine day, and have someone foot the ladder whilst you check gutters.

FRUIT-TREE SPRAYING

SCAB AND MILDEW
Controlled by thiophanate-methyl, benomyl or captan. Spray from bud burst until midsummer at four-week intervals

CATERPILLARS AND SAWFLY LARVAE
Controlled by fenitrothion. Spray a week after petal fall and twice in early summer at a fortnight's interval

plants

OF THE

month

MAHONIAS

The mahonias were once included in the Berberis genus, but were then recognised as a clearly distinct group worthy of independent status. Their close relationship is proved, however, by the existence of hybrids between the two genera, listed under the name × Mahoberberis. Try the cultivar 'Magic', a 'sit-up-and-beg', sturdy plant with well-armed holly-like foliage – but smaller.

MAHONIA × MEDIA 'CHARITY'

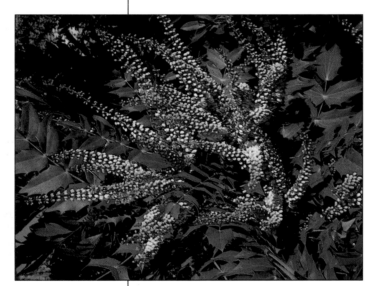

MAHONIA × WAGNERI 'MOSERI'

MAHONIA × MEDIA 'CHARITY'

type	Hardy, evergreen, upright shrub
size	Height 3.5m (12ft)
foliage	Decorative, flat pinnate leaves with approximately 13 spiny leaflets. Leaflets 6–15cm (2½–6in) long, leaves 30–45cm (12–18in)
flowers	Many 15–30cm (6–12in) spikes at the end of each branch, with lots of deep lemon, cup-shaped flowers opening in succession over many weeks and months, from mid-autumn through the winter. Very fragrant
site	Best out of the fiercest sun
soil	Good soil that does not dry out
care	Strong plant. Tends to want to grow like a palm tree, very erect. Tall plants can be severely cut down to a few inches, from which they will grow again
other cultivars	'Lionel Fortescue', 'Buckland', 'Winter Sun'. All are similar

MAHONIA × WAGNERI 'MOSERI'

type	Hardy, evergreen, low shrub, a hybrid of the common *M. aquifolium*
size	60cm–1m (2–3ft)
foliage	Flattish, serrated, tough leaves in various shades of matt pink and red throughout the year. A most attractive and reliable foliage shrub
flowers	Clenched fists of yellow blossom, perhaps late winter into spring
site	Whilst *Mahonia aquifolium* will grow reasonably in even the most derelict and difficult places, 'Moseri' is worth better things. However, it is not difficult, even in relatively poor soil
care	Do not crowd it as it can make a fine specimen. A steady rather than a rampant grower, so will probably never need pruning
propagation	Seed will give varied plants. Propagate with occasional suckers or by air layering
other cultivars	'Fireflame', 'Pinnacle'. 'Undulata' is a strong upright shrub with very dark green polished holly leaves that become bronzed in winter. Tight bunched golden flowers appear in spring

ILEX × ALTACLERENSIS 'GOLDEN KING'

HOLLIES FOR THE GARDEN

There are many forms, most of which are splendid. The 'Ferox' kinds have spines on the surface of the leaves, something that adds to their curiosity value, not their looks. Try:

'**J. C. Van Tol**', self-fertile, red-berried, good form
'**Golden Van Tol**', upright, dark leaves with irregular golden edges
'**Mme Briot**', wide, shining dark leaves bordered gold, red berries
'**Pyramidalis Fructo Luteo**', neat, dark column with some middle-age spread, leaves not very spiny, berries yellow

HOLLIES

Hollies are invaluable plants for hedging and for providing a wonderful background of evergreen colour for other shrubs and herbaceous plants. Few things are more windproof, so they are very useful for breaking the force of gales and providing welcome shelter. They come as males and females on separate plants; do not be misled by the given names, as 'Kings' can be female and 'Queens' male. Hollies grow more quickly than most gardeners believe: the twelve months after planting they can spend sizing up the situation and getting ready to surprise later.

◣ ILEX × ALTACLERENSIS 'GOLDEN KING'

type	Hardy, evergreen, shrub or tree. One of a group of hollies grouped under the name *Ilex × altaclerensis*, presumed hybrids from *I. aquifolium* (common holly) and others. Female
size	Height 6m (20ft), spread to 5m (16ft) but can be easily pruned to size
foliage	Handsome, large leaves with spines, but not so fierce as some. Dark polished green with a somewhat lighter centre, but boldly margined in gold. New growth pleasingly suffused purple
flowers and fruit	Usual discreet holly flowers followed by a rather meagre crop of tawny red berries
site	Makes a good specimen or can be pressed into service as a classy, bright and impenetrable hedge
soil	Any reasonable drained soil
care	Needs little attention bar perhaps pruning an occasional over-exuberant twig reaching out of its silhouette

ILEX AQUIFOLIUM 'ARGENTEA MARGINATA'

type	Hardy, evergreen shrub or tree. Female
size	Height 12m (40ft), spread 6m (20ft). Can be kept to required size by pruning
foliage	Polished, spiky, dark green foliage with creamy margins. Young leaves pinky-mauve
flowers and fruit	Small cream flowers followed by heavy crops of shining red berries
site	Undemanding. Makes a splendid specimen tree, but equally good for hedging
care	Splendid strong tree, needs no attention except to prune occasional stray branches

MAHONIAS TO TRY

A rather overlooked genus with over sixty forms in cultivation. Try:

M. aquifolium '**Smaragd**', very dark-leaved form
M. japonica, one of the parents of the hybrid 'Charity' and its siblings, splendid in its own right
M. pinnata, neat, upright shrub with small holly-like foliage

practical project

GROWING CLIMBING PLANTS AND CLOTHING WALLS

RECOMMENDED IVIES

Hedera algeriensis (canariensis), **'Gloire de Marengo',** large-leaved, dark green with silver-grey patches and strong white margins

Hedera colchica, **'Dentata Variegata',** large leathery leaves, green with irregular, bold golden variegation

H.c. **'Sulphur Heart' ('Paddy's Pride'),** striking, strong, big leaves of very dark green giving way to paler green around a starry central patch of yellow

Hedera helix **(common ivy):** **'Buttercup',** bright golden-yellow leaves, brightest in open light

'Glacier', smallish, well-pointed leaves in silver-grey and pale, dusky green

'Goldheart', popular, neat 3–5 pointed leaves, shining dark green around golden centres

'Sagittifolia', strong grower with lots of narrow, pointed, lobed leaves almost like talons

Over 350 forms of the common ivy are currently available – why not start a collection?

With today's smaller gardens, it makes sense to use the walls of the house as garden extensions. The warmth helps many, the support provides the habitat for many climbers and clamberers, and clothing the walls or parts of them will integrate the house with the garden and can enhance both the appearance and possibly the value of a property. Once planted and given the necessary support, if any, wall plants will repay you with trouble-free – and, in many cases, maintenance-free – colour and interest: throughout the year if you choose carefully.

WALL PLANTS

For convenience, wall plants can be divided into four groups: free-standing ones that enjoy the shelter; climbing ones with 'self-adhesive' devices; twiners seeking support by twisting around wires, trellis or other plants; and climbing and scrambling kinds needing definite support. Some of the flowering climbers are discussed on pp96–7; here we look at the four groups in more detail. (See also p140.)

Free-standing plants

At the base of a wall you can place plants that enjoy extra warmth and protection. These include the winter-flowering *Iris unguicularis*, autumn-flowering bulbous *Nerine bowdenii* and small-flowering gladioli such as the *G. nanus* cultivars. Then there are shrubs that are helped by the warmth of the wall: the quinces (*Chaenomeles*) hurried into early bloom, the camellias in cool areas, winter-flowering *Garrya elliptica* and *Chimonanthus praecox*, some of the Mediterranean plants and shrubs such as the Cistus species and hybrids, and the ceanothus, shrubs that are magnificent on a wall with their clouds of blue blossom. Further examples are listed in the margin.

Self-adhesive climbers

The obvious self-adhesive example is ivy. The common ivy, *Hedera helix*, has hundreds of cultivars, many with very bright variegation. They keep walls dry and warm and do no damage; good mortar will not be affected by ivy, which can only damage old, rotten mortar and then only when pulled off the wall. *H. colchica* and *H. algeriensis (canariensis)* are spectacular, large-leaved species. Again, further examples are listed in the margin.

The other popular suckering plants are those collectively known as Virginia creepers, though only *Parthenocissus quinquefolia*, with leaves composed of five leaflets, has a real right to the name. The most widespread of these

climbers is the Boston ivy, *P. tricuspata*, that can quickly cover large walls; mature leaves are broad and normally three lobed. Both make dense cover and turn brilliant colours before leaving themselves bare stemmed for the winter. They tend to be a little late into fresh growth. In the same mould are *P. henryana*, with leaves divided into five leaflets and attractively veined and suffused pink, and the rather bristly leaved *Ampelopsis brevipedunctata*.

Euonymus fortunei radicans is a dark evergreen; the large number of its boldly variegated cultivars such as 'Emerald and Gold' and 'Silver Queen' are useful to lighten up dark corners. Some of these are more bushy but can reach up with their backs against a wall; the type and some cultivars will root as they go and will climb to the bedroom windows.

Chimonanthus praecox

Twiners and twisters

Clematis species and hybrids, honeysuckles and *Celastrus orbiculatus* all fall into this group and are covered in some detail on pp96–7. Now is the time to prune *Clematis jackmanii* types. *Clematis armandii*, not discussed earlier, is an evergreen with dark, oval, lobed foliage and early flowers. If it finds support it will grow quickly up to 5–6m (16–20ft), but it is more effective kept rather lower where the frost-proof, wide white flowers 4–5cm (1½–2in) across can be better seen in early spring. 'Snowdrift' and the pale pink 'Appleblossom' are preferred cultivars.

The huge-leaved deciduous vine, *Vitus coignetiae*, is impressive; some leaves can be over 30cm (12in) across. With foliage widely heart shaped and roughly textured, it is opulent through the growing months and brilliant before leaf fall.

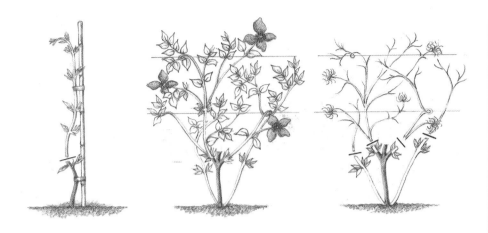

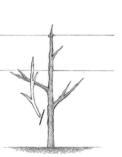

FREE-STANDING SHRUBS FOR WALLS

Abelia* × *grandiflorum, white and pink flowers, midsummer into autumn

Camellia, pink, red or white flowers, late winter and spring

Ceanothus, blue flowers, spring, summer and autumn, depending on cultivar

Chimonanthus praecox, wintersweet, shiny lemon and maroon flowers

Choisya ternata, Mexican orange blossom, white flowers, late spring and sometimes also autumn

***C. t.* 'Sundance'**, golden foliage

Cistus, rock roses, white, cream, yellow, orange, pink or red flowers, throughout summer

Crinodendron hookerianum, evergreen, crimson flowers, late spring and early summer, lime-free soil

Cytisus battandieri, giant Moroccan broom, huge grey leaves and pineapple-shaped and scented flower spikes, early and midsummer

Escallonia* × *iveyi, small dark green leaves, lots of white blossom in late summer and autumn

Itea ilicifolia, evergreen with polished holly leaves, ivory-white narrow 'catkins' hanging 23cm (9in) in late summer

Magnolia grandiflora, large-leaved evergreen, large, white fragrant flowers, midsummer into autumn

Osmanthus delavayi, dark evergreen, small white, fragrant funnel flowers

Pyracantha, various, creamy blossom, early summer, brilliant berries autumn and winter

(See p97 for Climbers for Shady Walls)

Scramblers

The winter jasmine has already been given good notices together with the potato-flowered *Solanum crispum* 'Glasnevin' (see p107). *Forsythia suspensa*, once widely grown, is these days undeservedly overlooked, possibly because it is not so blatant as its extrovert relations. It is a pleasing plant to grow up a wall with support, in the same way as one would the jasmine. Once helped to form a reasonable backbone, the lateral growth will arch down with uncrowded spring blossom of primrose yellow. Cut these branches back to two or so buds after flowering to give lots of fresh flowering wood for next spring – not too much of a chore.

Planting near walls

Although many climbing roses and other climbers planted tight against house walls do thrive, it makes better sense to plant 30–40cm (12–16in) away from the wall and lead the growing stems to the wall. Self-clingers will get growing more quickly if they are initially stuck to the wall with adhesive tape. Climbers and shrubs needing support can be secured to trellis fixed to the wall! The fixing of the trellis needs to be thoroughly done; it has to withstand gales that will catch the growing plants and create considerable tension. Strong trellis can be attached to the wall using a generous number of screws and rawlplugs.

Pruning climbers

Climbing-rose pruning has been dealt with on p20. Most other wall shrubs need relatively little pruning. Pyracanthas and euonymus can be clipped to shape quite strictly or allowed to grow more freely by simply cutting back leaning branches. Ceanothus can be similarly clipped. Winter jasmine and *Forsythia suspensa* will be encouraged to make new flowering wood if clipped back in spring when flowers have faded.

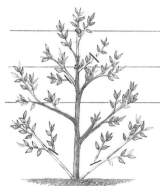

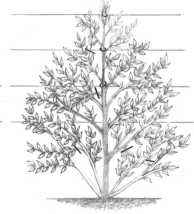

plants
OF THE
month

IVY

There is a lot more to ivy than the common one clinging to a tree trunk or old garden wall. There are literally hundreds of cultivars, many of which are variegated, helping them to look colourful even in the darkest days of winter. Some of these take on pink and mauve tints in the coldest weather and are worth looking at closely outside or bringing into the house for indoor decoration.

ELEPHANT'S EARS
Hedera colchica 'Dentata Variegata'

type	Hardy, evergreen, self-adhesive climber
size	Height 10m (30ft)
foliage	Large, wide, roughly heart-shaped leaves 8–20cm (3–8in) long. Tough, dark green with very generous creamy-yellow variegation
flowers	Normal ivy flowers but only on adult plants
site	On walls, large tress, fences or grown as a specimen in a tub or large container. Grown over even a skeleton fence this scrambling, clambering, character can give the impression of a very distinguished and trouble-free hedge
care	Strong plant, but newly installed ones get away quicker if their stems are tied closely to their support
propagation	Easiest by layering
related cultivars	*H. algeriensis* 'Gloire de Marengo', creamy variegation

GOLDEN IVY
Hedera helix 'Buttercup'

type	Hardy, evergreen, self-adhesive climber, a form of the common ivy
size	Height 6m (20ft)
foliage	Wide, pointed leaves of yellow-green and gold. In open sites the stronger gold is retained throughout the year
site	See above
care	Whilst the plant needs no more care than the common ivy to keep healthy – ie pure neglect – you can trim back the leaves periodically to keep fresh young foliage minted in purest shining gold. It is easier to do this if the ivy is grown over a low wall. See also margin
other varieties	See margin list on p132

ELEAGNUS PUNGENS 'MACULATA'

Many variegated plants turn up as mutations and then become more popular than the parent plant. This certainly applies to *Eleagnus pungens* 'Maculata'. It is so bright it could outdo the display of many flowering plants – and this throughout the year!

type	Hardy, evergreen shrub with occasional sharp spines
size	Height and spread 3–4m (9–12ft)
foliage	Tough, very glossy leaves, their dark green more or less confined to the margins as the main blade of the leaf is a rich gold. One of the best foliage shrubs, especially effective through the winter months
flowers	Not important, but one or two in leaf axils, silvery-white and perfumed, 1.25cm (½in) across. Mid- to late autumn

HEDERA HELIX 'BUTTERCUP'

site   Easy to grow in sun or shade
soil   Any reasonable soil
care   Little to do except to prune out cleanly any branch or twig which reverts to all-green leaves
propagation   By layering

FIRETHORN
(Pyracantha rogersiana flava)

type   Hardy, evergreen shrub usually grown for its decorative fruit
size   Height and spread 4m (12ft)
foliage   Dark green, oblong, polished
flowers   Clustered hawthorn-type white flowers in early summer, followed by heavy crops of golden berries. Many other cultivars from lemon-yellow to more frequent rich orange and red kinds
site   In the open with the initial support of a strong post, but more usually up a wall on wires or trellis
care   Prune to shape. Secure young plants to their wall support
propagation   By layering early summer to lift following late spring
other cultivars   *Pyracantha atalantioides*, red; P. a. 'aurea', palish gold; *P. coccinea* 'Lalandii', large, orange-red; 'Golden Charmer', golden-orange; 'Orange Glow', 'Soleil d'Or', golden; 'Teton', prolific, smallish, orange-red

SKIMMIA JAPONICA

Give this shrub the conditions suggested below and you will be rewarded with one of the most respectable and well-behaved of plants, which distinguishes itself in its female forms by carrying red berries almost all year round.

type   Hardy, evergreen shrub, mainly grown for its persistent berries
size   Height and spread 1.5m (5ft)
foliage   Tough, entire leaves like a small laurel, rich green
flowers   Tight clusters of tiny flowers in mid- to late spring. Female plants then produce heavy crops of shining red berries that persist – almost as good as plastic!
site   Best in light shade
soil   Fertile, moist soil
care   Foliage can become yellowish in very strong sunlight, in poor soils

SKIMMIA JAPONICA

or ones with an excess of lime, something which can be corrected with humus and/or sulphur chips. Plants are either male or female. For a female to berry there has to be a male planted fairly nearby. If a group are planted one male will fertilise five or six females
propagation   From cuttings in early summer or by layering
other forms   *Skimmia j. reevesiana* is a form with male and female flowers on the same plant; its berries are slightly smaller, somewhat more crimson and matt in finish; *S.j.* 'Rubella' is a densely-built upright shrub perhaps 1.5m (5ft) high but not so wide. Terminal flower buds make tight rounded red bunches. These deep red buds open into small white stars in spring. It is a male form; *S.j.* 'Fructualba' is an effective dark-leaved form with tight clusters of small white flowers followed by persistant pure white berries; *S.j.* 'Veitchii' is another robust upright shrub. Its clusters of little white flowers are followed by shining red berries. It has perhaps the largest leaves and berries; these can be round or pear-shaped

UNUSUAL BERRIES

Arbutus unedo, strawberry tree, orange-red lychees
Callicarpa bodinieri giraldii **'Profusion',** tight clusters of violet fruits
Celastrus orbiculatus, climber with black fruits splitting open to show gold and scarlet seeds
Euonymus europaeus, fleshy pink fruits opening to display orange seeds
Sorbus vilmorinii, rosy-red fruits becoming blush-white

AN UNUSUAL FEATURE
An alternative form of culture for ivies could be to take Hedera helix *'Buttercup' or another colourful cultivar and grow it up a strategically placed post. Tie in growing stems until the top is reached and then pinch out the growing points. The plant will then grow more thickly below until the post becomes a living pillar of colourful foliage, a beacon in the garden. If the foliage is trimmed once or twice a year fresh new leaves are encouraged and the brightest effect achieved.*

appendix
1

TREES FOR THE SMALLER GARDEN

Crataegus coccinea

Acer japonicum cv

Malus cv.

Acer griseum Maple with orange, flaking bark. Leaves of three leaflets turn red and orange in autumn

A. japonicum various Much-divided leaves, brilliant autumn colours. Slow growing

A. palmatum various Well over a hundred forms on sale with 5–7 pointed lobed leaves in greens and purples; autumn colours. Slow growing

A. pseudoplatanus 'Brilliantissimum' A sycamore, but relatively dwarf. Leaves very colourful, pink and cream

Arbutus × **andrachnoides** Steady rather than fast growing. A pleasing evergreen to 9m (30ft), with 'strawberry' fruits and white flowers from autumn through till spring

Betula utilis var. jacquemontii Makes an evenly proportioned tree with upward-reaching branches; bark a dazzling white

Cercis siliquastrum Judas tree, 5 x 3m (16 x 10ft) Hosts of purple-pink pea flowers in late spring. Rounded foliage. Very good for hot dry spots

Chamaecyparis lawsoniana 'Allumii' Slowish-growing, blue-green conifer

C.l. 'Lane' Good triangular form and a bright golden colour. One of the best

Cotoneaster × **watereri** 8 x 6m (26 x 20ft) Spreading evergreen with copious crops of persistent red berries in large clusters

Crataegus coccinea Scarlet hawthorn; typical hawthorn form with a wide head. Broad serrated leaves, late-spring blossom in wide, scarlet clusters

C. laevigata 'Paul's Scarlet' The red-flowered hawthorn. Dark green leaves, doubled pinky-red flowers in late spring to early summer

C. × **lavallei 'Carrierei'** 6–7m (20–23ft) Strong, sturdy tree with a wide head. Dark, tough, polished leaves, red in autumn. White flowers followed by large round fruits in golds, oranges and reds, held for months after the leaves have gone

Eucalyptus nicholii Modest-sized tree with very narrow, hanging leaves and slender red stems. A very graceful eucalypt

E. niphophila Very hardy. Spear-shaped hanging leaves, variously coloured trunk. New foliage orangey

Gleditsia triacanthus 'Sunburst' Deciduous; more or less horizontally branched. Cut foliage is fern-like, glowing soft yellow in spring, rather greener later

Ilex aquifolium 'J C van Tol' 6 x 4m (20 x 12ft) dark leaved holly that is unusually self-fertile. Alternatives are variegated kinds, see p131

Juniperus 'Skyrocket' 8m x 80cm (25ft x 30in) Very narrow column of blue green

Laburnum × **vossii** The most spectacular of laburnums with hanging tresses 40cm (16in) long of golden-yellow pea flowers, late spring and early summer

Malus floribunda A fine crab apple, with clouds of red-budded, pink-flowered blossom in mid- and late spring. Small yellowish 'apples' the size of peas in autumn

M. 'Lemoinei' Foliage reddish-purple, with age taking on a metallic-bronze hint. Spring blossom rich burgundy red followed by dark purple-red crab apples

M. 'Profusion' 7m (23ft) tall; a spreading tree. Young purple foliage rather greener later. Great quantities of glowing purplish-pink blossom in late spring. Dark, smallish crab apples in autumn

Morus nigra Black mulberry. Makes a rounded, characterful tree with large wide leaves and dark mulberries in the autumn. Dark green leaves turn golden before falling

Sorbus hupehensis

Parrotia persica Sprawling, falling, spreading tree with a squat trunk. Handsome dark foliage turns to many shades of gold, orange and purplish-red in autumn. Small red flowers appear in early spring just when it is getting ready to unfurl its new leaves

Prunus cerasifera 'Pissardii' Can make a rounded tree 10m (30ft) tall, turned into a cloud of pale pink in early and mid-spring before the new red foliage opens; leaves turn purple with age

P. subhirtella 'Autumnalis' Makes a wide, flat-headed tree with lots of semi-pendent branches. From leaf fall to the early spring it carries lots of small white or blush-pink blossom. One of the most reliable of winter flowers

P. 'Amanogawa' Strictly upright tree with large, semi-double, pale pink flowers in late spring

P. 'Kiku-shidare-zakura' Weeping tree with very pendent branches thickly wrapped around with clusters of doubled, rich pink blossom in mid- to late spring

P. 'Mount Fuji' ('Shirotae') Widely spreading tree with horizontal branches somewhat arching. Large snow white, scented flowers in mid-spring. Distinguished-looking specimen

P. 'Ukon' Makes a largish, spreading tree with many clusters of semi-double flowers opening pale greenish-cream from pinkish buds; can become pale blush-pink with age. Young bronzed leaves turn green

Pyrus salicifolia Willow-leaved silvery pear with somewhat pendent branches. White pear blossom amongst silver-grey foliage in spring. 6m (20ft)

Rhus typhina Stag's horn sumach, 5 x 6m (15 x 20ft) Is easily formed into small tree. Attractive large pinnate leaves with brilliant autumn colours. Interesting winter silhouette

Robinia pseudoacacia 'Frisia' The popular yellow-leaved false acacia. Pinnate leaves. Upright

Salix babylonica pekinensis 'Tortuosa' With corkscrewing branches and narrow, twisted leaves this is a character. Best planted where its habit of dropping twigs and leaves will not cause annoyance

S. daphnoides Grown for its purple stems, often covered with white plum-like bloom

Sorbus aria Whitebeam. Neat tree with silvery-white bursting leaf buds, grey-green leaves becoming dark with age. White flowers followed by rusty-red fruits

S. hupehensis Rowan-type tree with blue-green foliage that has rich autumn colours. The large bunches of fruit are white, blushing pale pink, and are as fine as any of the genus

S. vilmorinii One of the finest of trees for the small garden, a modest-sized tree of graceful outline with finely cut, small pinnate leaves that give it a ferny look. The clusters of early-summer white flowers are followed by lots of rosy fruits that turn white

Stuartia pseudocamellia 8 x 5m (28 x 16ft) Upright shrub with camellia-like, white late-summer flowers. Oval leaves become gold, orange and red in autumn

Styrax japonica Snowbell tree, 6 x 4m (20 x 12ft). Wide-reaching level branches are hung with early-summer white bells. Best in moist lime-free soil

Taxus baccata 'Fastigiata' Irish yew. Tight upright columns of dark foliage

T.b. 'Fastigiata Aureomarginata' A form of the erect Irish yew with leaves edged yellow

Parrotia persica

Robinia pseudoacacia

Taxus baccata

appendix

2

Abelia grandiflora More or less evergreen, making a rounded bush to 1.2m (4ft). Shiny, pointed oval leaves. Many clusters of pink and white scented flowers from midsummer until winter

Acer japonicum Slow-growing foliage maples. Rounded leaves but with 7–11 pointed lobes. 'Aureum is a lovely pale yellow form

A. palmatum Japanese maple with hundreds of forms. 'Dissectum Atropurpureum' is the dark form with filigree, divided leaves

Aralia elata 'Variegata' Wonderful foliage; pinnate leaves 1m (3ft) or more long and broadly variegated creamy-white

Arbutus unedo Strawberry tree. Dark, evergreen, tough leaves. White, large, heather-like flowers followed by rusty-red 'strawberry' fruits

A. × andrachnoides Similar to the last, fruits smaller; eventually a tree

Berberis darwinii Evergreen, tiny holly leaves, lots of golden-orange spring blossom

B. × stenophylla Evergreen with dark, narrow leaves, thick arching growth covered with deep golden blossom in spring

B. ×thunbergii Deciduous. Many forms, the most popular ones having foliage a rich burgundy purple

Brachyglottis 'Sunshine' Formerly *Senecio*. Evergreen silver-leaved bush that grows well in poor soils. Summer flowers are clusters of yellow daisies

Buddleia alternifolia Hanging, long slender branches wreathed with small lilac flowers in early summer

Camellia × williamsii 'Donation' Most famous of hybrids. Beautifully formed semi-double, rich pink large flowers in late winter and early spring. Healthy, shiny dark foliage

Ceanothus impressus One of many fine wall shrubs, with dark evergreen foliage lost in spring behind millions of rounded heads of blue flowers

Chimonanthus praecox Wintersweet. Deciduous. Mid- and late winter blossom of a limy-yellow with maroon centre. Highly fragrant. Best on a wall

Choisya ternata Mexican orange blossom, 1.5–2 x 1.8–2.5m (5–6 x 6–8ft) rounded evergreen with scented bunches of white flowers in spring

Cistus × purpureus Rounded evergreen shrub 1.2m (4ft) tall with narrow, rough-textured leaves and midsummer flowers 8cm (3in) across, showy deep pink with dark basal spots

Corylopsis pauciflora 1.2–1.5m (4–5ft) spreading deciduous shrub with lots of stubby, primrose-coloured catkins in late winter

C. spicata Like the last, but with longer, limy catkins in early spring

Cotinus coggygria Smoke bush. Deciduous, rounded green leaves, but with very deep purple forms such as 'Royal Purple'. Much divided flowerheads make 'smoky' plumes

Cytisus kewensis Prostrate broom. Pale yellow blossom in spring

Deutzia × elegantissima 'Rosealind' 1 x 1.5m (3 x 5ft) deciduous round bush, fresh green leaves, large clusters deep pink blossom in late spring, early summer

Escallonia macrantha Evergreen up to 3m (9ft). Dense, dark green mass background for the rich red flowers, freely produced from early summer onwards

Genista hispanica Spanish gorse. 30–45cm (12–18in) tall, dense, rounded green spiny mass covered in gold flowers in late spring to early summer

MORE RECOMMENDED SHRUBS

Camellia x williamsii 'Donation'

Cotinus coggygria 'Flame'

Abelia grandiflora

G. lydia Spreading, low shrub that becomes a complete mass of gold in late spring and early summer. Sunny spot

Halesia carolina Snowdrop tree. Grows from shrub to tree up to 6m (20ft). Deciduous. Somewhat hanging stems strung with pure white 'snowdrop' bells in late spring

Hebe speciosa 'Midsummer Beauty' 2 x 1.5m (6 x 5ft). Evergreen, bright green leaves, maroon below. Many long lilac spikes fading to white from midsummer to late autumn

Itea ilicifolia 3 x 3m (10 x 10ft). Evergreen, arching stems with dark holly-like foliage. Hung with long slender pale yellow catkins in late summer and autumn

Jasminum nudiflorum Indispensable winter jasmine. Dark leaves with current year's wood also dark green. Scrambling shrub that can be pinned up to a wall or allowed to fall down a bank. Yellow blossom from autumn through winter

Jasminium nudiflorum

Vitis cognetiae

Pieris formosa forrestii

Magnolia stellata Star magnolia, 3 x 4m (10 x 12ft). Deciduous, intricate shrub. Many-petalled white flowers before and as narrow leaves begin to unfurl in early to mid-spring

Olearia haastii Sturdy rounded evergreen bush, 1.2–2.5m (4–9ft). Dark foliage as a background for clusters of small white daisy flowers through the summer

Osmanthus delavayi Neat, evergreen, small polished leaves. Arching stems become loaded with flower buds in winter. They open in spring, shining white and very fragrant

Philadelphus 'Belle Etoile' One of the highly scented 'mock oranges', an arching deciduous shrub up to 1.5m (5ft). Lots of white flowers with central maroon spot and boss of anthers in late spring and early summer

Pieris formosa forrestii Evergreen with brilliant red and orange young foliage which turns pink and/or cream before becoming green. Spring and early summer racemes of white flowers

Prunus × cistena In early spring the dark stems clasp lots of wide, white flowers. Then comes the shiny purple-red foliage. A 2m (6ft) tall bush that can be used for hedging

Rosa banksia lutea Tall climbing rose with glorious wide, single, rich yellow flowers. Best in warmer areas

R. gallica versicolor *Rosa mundi.* The old bushy rose with flat, open, semi-double flowers of pink tellingly overpainted by red splashes pointing to the centres

Salix lanata Neat bush perhaps up to 60cm (2ft) high and 1m (3ft) wide. Wide, rounded grey leaves, silver in youth. The male has large, rounded, upright golden catkins

Sambucus racemosa 'Plumosa Aurea' Red-berried elder, 3 x 3m (10 x 10ft) deciduous. Grown for its masses of ferny, divided rich golden leaves

Spiraea 'Arguta' Bridal wreath. Arching bush of many stems. In mid- and late spring masses of shining white blossom cover the length of each stem 1.2m (3–6ft)

S. thunbergii Arching deciduous shrub, with clusters of small white flowers in early and mid-spring. Rather pale green leaves become vivid red before dropping

S. × vanhouttei Like 'Arguta' but taller, large bush

Ulex europaeus 'Flore Pleno' Double gorse, 1 x 1.2m (3 x 4ft) tight hedgehog bush of dark green spikes. Covered overall with double golden, scented flower in spring

Vitis coignetiae The largest-leaved vine, will climb to almost any heights. Impressive, wide leaves often 25cm (10in) across. Rich autumn colours

Prunus x cistena

appendix

3

Abutilon megapotamicum 1.8–3m (6–10ft). Evergreen to train against a warm wall. Oval dark green leaves, large hanging bells of yellow and red in succession from late spring to autumn

Actinidia chinensis Kiwi fruit. Strong, heart-shaped, rough-textured leaves, coffee-coloured flowers like small single roses. Plants of both sexes needed for fruit

Akebia quinata Chocolate vine, 9–12m (30–40ft). Twiner, semi-evergreen in mild spots. Leaves of five oval leaflets, hanging clusters of rounded vanilla-scented brown-purple flowers in late spring. Long finger purple fruits

Aristolochia durior Dutchman's pipe, 6–8m (20–26ft). Twiner. Big heart-shaped leaves, pipe-flowers of shades of yellow, brown and green in early summer

MORE FLOWERING CLIMBERS

Billardiera longiflora 2m (6ft). Evergreen twiner; narrow dark green leaves; small limy or purple tinged bells in summer followed by unusual hanging purple-blue fruits in autumn

Campsis radicans Trumpet vine, 12m (40ft). Deciduous clinger for warm wall. Leaves like wisteria's of many leaflets, light green. Small bunches of trumpet flowers in yellow, orange and red, each 6–8cm (2½–3in) long in late summer and autumn

Celastrus orbiculatus Strong twiner; when both sexes are planted it is very decorative with lots of yellow and red fruits. Yellow foliage for autumn colour. Needs lots of room

Humulus lupulus 'Aureus' Golden hop, 6m (20ft). Herbaceous twiner with limy-yellow foliage. Leaves divided into three or five lobes. Greenish-primrose typical hanging hop flowers in autumn

Jasminum officinalis Common white jasmine. Long shoots clamber over any support. Good quantities of sweet-scented white blossom through the summer months

Jasminum officinale

Passiflora caerulea Passion flower. In warm spots this can survive the winter, especially if the bottom 60cm (2ft) is given some protection against the worst of the frost. The fascinating flowers some 10cm (4in) across must be worth this little chore

Pileostegia viburnoides Aerial roots make it self clinging. An evergreen with long, pointed, almost laurel-like leaves and in late summer through autumn many much-branched panicles of small, creamy-white flowers with protruding stamens producing a light, pleasing effect. Closely related to the hydrangeas and schizophragmas but with all flowers fertile, ie no infertile, bract-like blossoms

Roses On warm walls flowers of the early kinds can be opening whilst daffodils are still about; later kinds will carry a long succession of bloom. They make excellent climbing frames for other plants, so that colourful blooming can cover a long period. Yellow 'Mermaid', salmon-pink 'Albertine', golden-yellow 'Golden Showers', crimson 'Parkdirektor Riggers' and lively pink 'Zephirine Drouhin' are established kinds that ought to be considered

Schizophragma hydrangeoides Japanese hydrangea vine. Self-clinging, deciduous plant, almost a look-alike for *Hydrangea petiolaris*, with the same type of loose, creamy lace-cap flowers

S. integrifolium Similar in growth to the last and with similar heart-shaped leaves. Flat summer heads of flowers, tiny fertile ones with marginal infertile pointing-finger bracts of cream

Pileostegia viburnoides

USEFUL ADDRESSES

Royal Horticultural Society
80 Vincent Square
London
SW1P 2PE

_____

Alpine Garden Society
AGS Centre
Avon Bank
Pershore
Worcestershire
WR10 3JP

_____

Hardy Plant Society
Administrator, Mrs Tricia King
Bank Cottage
Great Comberton
Worcestershire
WR10 3DP

_____

National Council for the
Conservation of
Plants and Gardens
The Pines
Wisley Garden
Woking
Surrey
GU23 6QB

_____

National Trust
PO Box 39
Bromley
Kent
BR1 1NH

_____

USA
American Horticultural Society
7931 East Boulevard Drive
Alexandria
Virginia 22308
tel. (703) 7685700

_____

CONVERSION TABLES

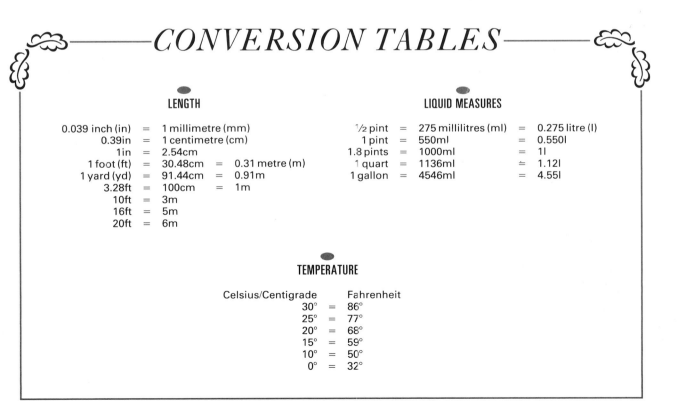

LENGTH

0.039 inch (in)	=	1 millimetre (mm)		
0.39in	=	1 centimetre (cm)		
1in	=	2.54cm		
1 foot (ft)	=	30.48cm	=	0.31 metre (m)
1 yard (yd)	=	91.44cm	=	0.91m
3.28ft	=	100cm	=	1m
10ft	=	3m		
16ft	=	5m		
20ft	=	6m		

LIQUID MEASURES

½ pint	=	275 millilitres (ml)	=	0.275 litre (l)
1 pint	=	550ml	=	0.550l
1.8 pints	=	1000ml	=	1l
1 quart	=	1136ml	≑	1.12l
1 gallon	=	4546ml	=	4.55l

TEMPERATURE

Celsius/Centigrade		Fahrenheit
30°	=	86°
25°	=	77°
20°	=	68°
15°	=	59°
10°	=	50°
0°	=	32°

FURTHER READING

The Plantfinder, RHS, Vincent Square, London SW1P 2PE. Lists plants in commerce and where you can buy them.

The Wildlife Garden Month by Month, Jackie Bennett, David & Charles, Newton Abbot, Devon. Shows how the garden may be a haven for wildlife.

RHS Gardeners' Encyclopedia of Plants and Flowers, 400pp of many illustrations, 200pp comprehensive text. A very worthwhile reference book.

Gardens of England and Wales, ('The Yellow Book') published annually by the National Gardens Scheme Charitable Trust. A guide to open days at over 3000 private gardens, the majority of which are not normally open to the public.

The Year-Round Bulb Garden, Brian Mathew, Souvenir Press. Deals with wide variety of bulbs hardy in temperate regions.

Hilliers Manual of Trees and Shrubs, David & Charles. Comprehensive listing of kinds available to gardeners.

The Small Garden, John Brookes, Aura Books. Full of design ideas for the less-than-large garden.

A History of British Gardening, Miles Hadfield. To dig into on a rainy day to learn how our forebears flexed their muscles. Also of interest to non-British gardeners.

Trees and Shrubs Hardy in the British Isles. Original text W J Bean, now updated. The bible of tree and shrub lovers. Expensive to buy all volumes but can be consulted in a good library.

ACKNOWLEDGEMENTS

No book is produced in isolation. Gardening books are not quite self-generating. Few are completely the sole work of one person. I enjoy gardening and its literature, new and old; sometimes the new is a bit different from the older and I expect it all exerts an influence. The text of this book, one of a practical series, has been my responsibility but the overall design has been the work of the David and Charles team. Jo Weeks at D & C has acted as midwife to this volume. Thank you Jo.

INDEX

Numbers in **bold** indicate main entry